Everyday Epiphanies

Everyday Epiphanies

MEETING CHRIST IN THE ORDINARY MOMENTS OF LIFE

JAMES A. HARNISH

ABINGDON PRESS | NASHVILLE

Everyday Epiphanies
Meeting Christ in the Ordinary Moments of Life

Copyright © 2025 Abingdon Press
All rights reserved.

No part of this work may be reproduced or transmitted in any form or by any means, electronic or mechanical, including photocopying and recording, or by any information storage or retrieval system, except as may be expressly permitted by the 1976 Copyright Act, the 1998 Digital Millennium Copyright Act, or in writing from the publisher. Requests for permission can be addressed to Rights and Permissions, The United Methodist Publishing House, 810 12th Avenue South, Nashville, TN 37203-4704 or emailed to permissions@abingdonpress.com.

Library of Congress Control Number: 2025935402
978-1-7910-3573-0

Scripture quotations unless noted otherwise are taken from the Common English Bible, copyright © 2011. Used by permission. All rights reserved.

Scripture quotations marked NRSVue are taken from the New Revised Standard Version, Updated Edition. Copyright © 2021 National Council of Churches of Christ in the United States of America. Used by permission. All rights reserved worldwide.

Scripture quotations marked KJV are taken from the Authorized (King James) Version. Rights in the Authorized Version in the United Kingdom are vested in the Crown. Reproduced by permission of the Crown's patentee, Cambridge University Press.

Scripture quotations marked MSG are taken from THE MESSAGE, copyright © 1993, 1994, 1995, 1996, 2000, 2001, 2002 by Eugene H. Peterson. Used by permission of NavPress. All rights reserved. Represented by Tyndale House Publishers, Inc.

Scripture quotations marked JBP are taken from The New Testament in Modern English by J. B. Phillips, copyright © 1960, 1972 J. B. Phillips. Administered by The Archbishops' Council of the Church of England. Used by Permission.

Scripture quotations marked CJB are taken from the Complete Jewish Bible by David H. Stern, copyright © 1998. Used by permission of Messianic Jewish Publishers.

MANUFACTURED IN THE UNITED STATES OF AMERICA

Earth's crammed with heaven,
And every common bush afire with God;
But only he who sees takes off his shoes;
The rest sit round it and pluck blackberries.
—Elizabeth Barrett Browning, *Aurora Leigh*

CONTENTS

Invitation ix

1 Catch Light on the Run 1

2 Old Eyes and New Visions 17

3 Meeting Christ in Dark Places 33

4 Remember Who You Are (And Who You Will Become) 47

5 New Wine at the Wedding 65

6 Turning the World Upside Down 81

7 Wake Up to Glory 99

Epilogue (Ash Wednesday): Remember You Are Dust 119

Notes 127

INVITATION

The Epiphany still happens. Ordinary people experience an extraordinary awareness of God's presence in unexpected places. It is a surprising gift in a specific moment in time that transforms the times that follow. The Epiphany can happen for you!

Epiphany is not a word we hear while standing around the coffeepot in the office, working out in the gym, or waiting in the pickup line at the elementary school.

The word sometimes carries a whiff of something bizarre, strange, even weird. It may suggest an esoteric experience for people who are not at all like the rest of us who live our ordinary lives in our ordinary world.

Epiphanies are not necessarily religious. Maya Angelou said that Epiphany "probably has a million definitions. It's the occurrence when the mind, the body, the heart, and the soul focus together and see an old thing in a new way."[1]

Epiphanies take us by surprise when we notice something we might have easily missed. They are not something we create or control. They uncover or reveal a new insight that helps us understand our past. They affect the way we live in the present and shape the way we live into the future.

I love the classic stories of Sir Isaac Newton's epiphany about gravity when an apple fell on his head or Archimedes running naked

Invitation

through the streets shouting "Eureka!" because he realized the principle of buoyancy when his bathtub overflowed. Those epiphanies are real. They are important in their own way. This book, however, is not about the general, all-purpose, or scientific kinds of epiphany. My interest is in the Epiphany in which we discover the presence of the God revealed in the life, death, and resurrection of Jesus Christ as a transformative reality in unexpected places in our otherwise ordinary lives.

In the Western church, the Epiphany commemorates the manifestation of Christ to the Gentiles by retelling Matthew's intriguing story of the coming of the magi. Three Kings' Day continues the tradition in parts of the world where the Roman Catholic Church maintains a cultural influence. In the Eastern (Orthodox) tradition, Epiphany commemorates the baptism of the Lord. This is the reason Greek boys in Tarpon Springs, Florida, have been celebrating the day with the custom of diving for the cross in Spring Bayou for 119 years. Protestants weave the two biblical stories together…if they recognize Epiphany at all!

Historian and author Diana Butler Bass awarded Epiphany the dubious honor of being "the most undervalued" season of the Christian year. It is often nothing more than the vacant space to catch our breath between the joyful celebration of Christmas and the somber days of Ash Wednesday and Lent. Bass's article surprised me with the insight that "Epiphany is about seeing the extraordinary in the everyday.… The mundane is charged with meaning—and epiphanies are everywhere."[2] Her words inspired both the title and the theme of this book.

My grounding conviction is that the Epiphany still happens when we experience the extraordinary presence of Christ in the ordinary patterns of our lives. Sometimes the Epiphany comes as a disturbing awareness of something that goes beyond our capacity to create or explain. Sometimes it awakens us to stand in opposition to the evils of racism, economic injustice, and violence around us. Sometimes it will "dawn upon us," as Zechariah described it.

> *Because of our God's deep compassion,*
> *the dawn from heaven will break upon us,*
> *to give light to those who are sitting in darkness*
> *and in the shadow of death,*
> *to guide us on the path of peace.*
> (Luke 1:78-79)

Sometimes we meet Christ in sun-soaked moments of explosive joy or in the dark shadows of disappointment, pain, or loss. The Epiphany can happen almost anytime, anywhere. It always calls us to do something in response to what we experienced.

Epiphany, like every season in the church calendar, is deeply rooted in scripture. The lectionary (the calendar of biblical texts we read in worship) provides readings that reverberate with wonder, confusion, and mystery in the revelation of the glory of God in Christ. Some of these stories are beautiful while some are downright bizarre. As we live into some of the Gospel stories, I invite you to watch for moments when you exclaim, "Hey! That's me! That's my story!" I also encourage you to share your epiphanies with trusted friends in a small group where others can share their stories and help confirm or refine your own.

I identify with Tennyson's words, in the voice of Ulysses: "I am a part of all that I have met."[3] I am part of an amazing array of people through whose lives and words I have seen the revelation of God's love made flesh in Jesus becoming flesh among us. Foremost among them, of course, is my wife, Martha, who read, edited, and improved this book. She is consistently a faithful person through whose life Christ is revealed in beautiful ways.

I offer this book in the spirit of the writer of the First Epistle of John.

Invitation

> We announce to you what...we have heard, what we have seen with our eyes, what we have seen and our hands handled, about the word of life.... What we have seen and heard, we also announce it to you so that you can have fellowship with us.... We are writing these things so that our joy can be complete.
>
> (1 John 1:1-4)

The Epiphany still happens! I pray it will happen for you!

Epiphany, January 6, 2025

CATCH LIGHT ON THE RUN

Matthew 2:1-12

I don't have the faintest idea how my GPS works. I'm totally baffled by the concept of a perfectly coordinated constellation of satellites that I will never find in the night sky but which find me wherever I am, pick up the direction I'm going, and set me on the best route to reach my destination. I still make wrong turns and get off course almost as often as I did in the old days, when my wife and I navigated with a paper map. Our marriage somehow survived the way she would fold the map back on itself while I insisted that it be folded neatly, the way we received it. It didn't help that in stereotypically misdirected male pride, I refused to ask for directions until we had no other option. I didn't want to confess that I needed help from someone who knew what I didn't know. GPS may have helped save our marriage!

I am even more flabbergasted when I imagine the way those satellites not only find and direct me but also are doing the same thing for millions of individuals all around the globe at the same time. GPS finds, knows, and leads the way for anyone anywhere who connects to the system and is open to its guidance. It's all a mind-bending mystery to me, but I've learned to trust it. It's become an ordinary part of my life, and I wouldn't leave home without it.

OnStar is one of the best-known GPS systems. And it makes the comparison to the star-gazing magi in Matthew's enigmatic story too good to pass up. They are the leading actors in the opening scene of the Epiphany drama. Their story also describes the way the Epiphany of Christ happens in many of our lives. The extraordinary "revelation" or "uncovering" of the presence of Christ is not something we create or control. It is always a gift. Sometimes it comes as an utterly unexpected surprise. The magi, however, would suggest that more often, Epiphany happens for people who are prepared to see, willing to follow, and open to surprises along the way.

"We've seen his star." (Matthew 2:2)

Decades ago, I found (or was I found by?) a story that hooked my attention and has never let go. It provides the title of this chapter.

In 1914, a fourteen-year-old boy in San Francisco received a box camera in preparation for a trip to Yosemite National Park. That ordinary gift opened Ansel Adams's eyes to the beauty and majesty of our wilderness. It led him to become America's best-known nature photographer.

Adams's autobiography includes his account of the experience that resulted in his famous photograph "Moonrise, Hernandez, New Mexico." The sun was setting when Adams caught a glimpse of the moon rising on the horizon. As he rushed to set up his camera, he shouted to his team, "Get that, for God's sake! We don't have much time!" When Richard Lacayo reviewed Adams's autobiography, he wrote, "Not much but enough for an artist of sublime sensibility to catch light on the run and keep it forever."[1]

The magi didn't have much to go on, just a new star that caught their attention when they were gazing into the night sky. It wasn't much, but it was enough to intrigue a few stargazers whose eyes had been trained to notice such things. They had a "sublime sensitivity to catch light on the run" and to follow it wherever it would lead them. You might say the star found them in the ordinary place of their ordinary lives and drew them to follow it in an extraordinary direction.

When it comes to their story, we don't have much to go on either. Despite the beautiful traditions that have accumulated around twelve verses in the beginning of Matthew's Gospel, there's more we don't know than we do know. The story is filled with mystery.

We don't know who they were. The Greek word *magoi* suggests priestly sages, astrologers, experts in studying the stars and interpreting dreams. Their identity as "kings" developed during the second century as the church told their story in the context of the Old Testament prophecy, "Nations shall come to your light, / and kings to the brightness of your dawn" (Isaiah 60:3 NRSVue). An eighth-century Irish tradition imagined them as representatives of three stages of life: youth, middle age, and old age. Over time, they received racial characteristics representing Europe, Africa, and Asia—the three regions of the world known by inheritors of this tradition. They were assigned different names depending on the culture in which the story was passed on.

We don't know exactly where they came from. "The East" is a big place! To borrow the name of a popular Broadway musical, they "come from away." The point is that they were Gentiles, foreigners, outsiders to God's covenant with the Hebrews.

We don't know how many there were. The assumption that there were three of them is based on the gifts they brought. Various traditions suggest as few as two and as many as twelve.

We don't know when they showed up. Despite the way we carefully position them with their camels around the manger, Matthew indicates that they came to the "house" where Mary, Joseph, and the baby were staying (2:11). Herod's infanticide of boys in Bethlehem younger than two years old suggests they arrived two years after Jesus's birth.

We don't even know if the story literally happened. Because there is no external record of the event, some biblical scholars believe Matthew's Gospel includes the story for a theological rather than historical purpose.

The "eureka" moment for me in revisiting the story is how extravagantly inclusive it is. Matthew tracks the genealogy of Jesus back to Abraham, clearly rooting him in the Hebrew tradition. But the coming of the magi breaks through the boundary between Jew and Gentile. It stretches any narrow religious or ethnic assumptions to see the revelation of Christ in the light of the extravagantly expansive prophetic visions of the Old Testament.

> *Let all the kings bow down before him;*
> *let all the nations serve him.*
> *Let it be so, because he delivers the needy who cry out,*
> *the poor, and those who have no helper.*
> *(Psalm 72:11-12)*

For Matthew, the coming of the magi sets in motion the drama that will reach its grand finale when, like the magi following the star, the disciples arrive at the mountain "to which Jesus had directed them." You could call it GPS—God's Positioning System. The story that begins with the surprising arrival of people who had no business being there concludes with Jesus's radically inclusive commission to his disciples at the Ascension.

> *I've received all authority in heaven and on earth. Therefore, go and make disciples of all nations, baptizing them in the name of the Father and of the Son and of the Holy Spirit, teaching them to obey everything that I've commanded you.*
> *(Matthew 28:18-20)*

The magi set our spiritual GPS toward Pentecost, when people "from every nation under heaven" hear the good news "in their native languages" (Acts 2:5-6). They prepare the way for Peter's epiphany that "God doesn't show partiality to one group of people over another" (Acts 10:34). The star they followed lifts our eyes to imagine "a great crowd that no one could number...from every nation, tribe, people, and language...standing before the throne and before the Lamb" (Revelation 7:9).

But I've rushed ahead of the story! The Mountain of the Ascension may be where Matthew's Gospel will end, but it's not where the story begins. It begins with the magi peering into the dark sky. Watching the stars was the ordinary pattern of their lives, just the way photography was the ordinary pattern of Ansel Adams's life. Their eyes were prepared to "catch light on the run" when they saw it and rise to follow. These strange visitors portray the way many of our faith stories begin. We may not have much to go on, but we have enough to catch a glimpse of the light of Christ and follow where it leads us. That is, at least, the way it's often been for me.

"Your word is a lamp to my feet and a light to my path." (Psalm 119:105 NRSVue)

I've never experienced the Epiphany as the sudden blaze of light like the one that knocked Saul off his horse on the Damascus road and blinded him for three days (Acts 9:1-9). I grew up hearing soul-stirring, evangelistic sermons about our individual need for a Damascus road experience. I looked for it, even prayed for it. If that's your experience, I celebrate it with you. But I never experienced Saul's identity-changing epiphany on the Damascus road.

I've experienced inspiring moments as I watched the changing shadows over the Great Smoky Mountains, when I saw the sun set over the Gulf of Mexico, or when I waited for the clouds to rise over

Table Mountain in Cape Town. I've been lifted beyond myself in the Spirit-soaked silence of the Washington National Cathedral, in singing around a youth campfire, or in the soaring melodies of powerful music. I've caught sight of the light of Christ in the twinkle in the eye of a baby being baptized and in the closing eyes of an aging saint. I've been challenged to more faithful discipleship by prophetic voices calling for freedom, justice, and peace.

I have not, however, borne witness to one instantaneously life-transforming epiphany that redirected my path in a different direction. The example of Paul's young protégé, Timothy, has been a liberating epiphany for me. There's no record that he experienced a blinding revelation of Christ. Instead, Paul told him to "rekindle the gift of God" he received from his mother, Eunice, and his grandmother, Lois (2 Timothy 1:6 NRSVue). Like Timothy, I received the gift of faith from my grandmother, Helena, my grandfather, Emerson, my mother, Randalyn, and my father, Sylvester. I can identify with John and Charles Wesley, who inherited the gift of faith from their parents, particularly their mother, Susanna. The Methodist movement was born when the spirit of God "rekindled" the fire of faith that was birthed within them in their childhood, nurtured by the Holy Club as students at Oxford, shattered by their failure as missionaries to Georgia, and enflamed by John Wesley's "heartwarming" epiphany at Aldersgate.

In the Wesleyan tradition, we call that gift prevenient grace. It's the undeserved grace of God that goes before our response and prepares us for the next step along the way. It's the love of God that finds us wherever we are but loves us too much to leave us there. It's the light of a star that leads us from where we are to the place we most deeply long to be.

The gift of faith I received from my parents and the church community in which I was raised prepared me for commitment services at summer youth camps and the altar calls at an old-fashioned camp meeting. In one of those settings, we spread our blankets on the grass of a rolling hillside in central Pennsylvania. We ended each service by singing the same song each time as we made our way back down the hillside into the camp.

> Follow I will follow Thee, my Lord,
> Follow every passing day.[2]

The best I can say about my faith is that I've been following its path ever since those formative experiences. Sometimes I've followed it with more clarity than others. There have been twists, turns, and detours as well as unexpected discoveries. I made wrong turns that required redirection. I found wise traveling companions who encouraged, challenged, and guided me when I might have settled down in some comfortable way station along the path.

One of those wise friends introduced me to the work of William Stafford, the one-time United States poet laureate (1970–71). His poem "The Way It Is" has become one of the guideposts for my life. He describes an unchanging thread that you can follow through all the tests and trials of life. He offers the assurance, "While you hold it you can't get lost.... You don't ever let go of that thread."[3] Those early decisions to follow Christ became the thread I've followed. It is the star that has guided me all the way.

My observation is that when it comes to the faith, most of us some of the time and some of us most of the time are like the magi. We may not have much to go on. We may not have been blinded by the light, but what we have is enough for us to catch sight of the light of Christ. Living by faith involves taking the next appropriate step with the light we've seen as we keep watching for fresh epiphanies along the way. The psalmist described it as a light for our path. It's just enough light to show us the next step to follow.

A conversation in a college dorm room with a fellow student and a wise mentor became a model for me of the life of faith. My friend was struggling with his commitment to follow Christ. He asked, "How can I make a commitment when I don't know everything it's going to mean?" I still hear the voice of our "wise man" when he replied, "None of us know everything it is going to mean. But we know enough to make the commitment, and we spend the rest of our lives finding out what it will mean." That conversation was nearly sixty years ago, but I've never improved on it. We sing it in John Greenleaf Whittier's words:

> In simple trust like theirs who heard
> beside the Syrian sea
> the gracious calling of the Lord,
> let us, like them, without a word
> rise up and follow thee.[4]

"They asked, 'Where is the newborn king of the Jews?'" (Matthew 2:2)

The magi were wise enough to know what they didn't know. In contrast to my resistance to asking for directions, they were willing to acknowledge when they had reached the end of their knowledge and needed more wisdom to guide them through the unknown present toward a hoped-for future.

The unknown is a tough place to be. I've never known anyone who enjoyed feeling lost, confused, or disoriented. It's frightening to feel our loss of control. In our strongly individualized culture, we'd rather sing with Frank Sinatra, "I did it my way." By contrast, former Archbishop of Canterbury Rowan Williams encourages us to "quarry through moments of strangeness and even disorientation…those moments when we don't quite know what is going on or what is happening in us." He calls us to "allow our unknowing to lead us to a place of deeper knowing."[5] When we find ourselves in those strange places, wise people search for deeper wisdom beyond their own. They ask for directions from others who have followed the star before them.

On one hand, there is a naive simplicity in the decision of the magi to go to the obvious place to ask for directions. They headed directly for King Herod's court in Jerusalem. If they were looking for the King of the Jews, what better place could they go to find him?

On the other hand, I'm struck by their courage in going to Herod. Kings, autocrats, and dictators in every age do not take kindly to anyone who threatens their power. The magi must have heard about the way Herod rid himself of anyone who threatened his reign, including members of his own family. As we will see later, it's an understatement for Matthew to say Herod was "troubled, and everyone in Jerusalem was troubled with him" (Matthew 2:3). Even Herod knew enough to know what he didn't know. He knew enough to turn to the Hebrew scriptures, which were evidently an unfamiliar source of wisdom for him. He called on scholars who searched in the past to find direction for the future. They found it in the tradition going all the way back to David and expressed by the prophet Micah.

> *As for you, Bethlehem of Ephrathah,*
>   *though you are the least significant of Judah's forces,*
>   *one who is to be a ruler in Israel on my behalf will come out*
>   *from you.*
>   *His origin is from remote times, from ancient days.*
>   (Micah 5:2)

If we're watching for the Epiphany of Christ, how would we know if we experienced it? The only way to identify the Epiphany of Christ is to experience it in ways that are consistent with the prophetic promises of the written word and the gospel witness of the Word made flesh in Jesus. We train our eyes to recognize the Epiphany as we live into the words of scripture and practice the spiritual disciplines of worship and prayer. We learn to see Christ by seeing how others have seen him across the long history of the faith.

Don't miss this. The magi and Herod read the same scripture. The magi were looking for the newborn king to honor him. Herod read the same texts to destroy him. It's a painful reminder that the Bible can be used to defend just about anything anyone intends to do. I'm writing in a time of profound social and political polarization. Some of the loudest voices in the American culture come from leaders who claim to hold a "biblical worldview." Oddly enough, that understanding often ends up being a version of Christian nationalism that is disturbingly consistent with a white, patriarchal, nationalistic way of seeing the world. It's a heretical worldview that fails to see the prophets' calls for justice for the poor or welcome for immigrants. It misses the pervasive biblical theme of caring for the creation. It glosses over some of the most disturbing words from Jesus and leaps past the Sermon on the Mount. The people who insist on posting the Ten Commandments in classrooms never suggest posting the Beatitudes.

If we're looking for the Epiphany of Christ, we'll recognize it when we find something that looks like the Word that became flesh in Jesus becoming flesh in the lives of ordinary people in ordinary places. It will look like the answer to our prayer that God's kingdom, as defined by the will, words, and way of Jesus, will come on earth as it is already fulfilled in heaven. It will be a way of living that produces "love, joy, peace, patience, kindness, goodness, faithfulness, gentleness, and self-control" (Galatians 5:22-23).

Herod and the magi found the direction they needed, but they found it for radically different purposes. The violence that lurks in the shadow of Herod's attempt to manipulate the magi will be uncovered in the ghastly story that follows. Matthew frames the gospel in the context of the ongoing tension between the ruling powers of this world and coming of the kingdom of God. That tension will eventually nail the king the magi sought to a cross.

"When they saw the star, they were filled with joy." (Matthew 2:10)

The most appropriate response to the Epiphany is awe-filled joy. Awe because it is not self-made. It is a wonder-filled gift. We catch a glimpse of a mystery that is beyond our powers of explanation but not beyond our experience. That's why the lectionary readings for Epiphany include Paul's mind-blowing affirmation of "the mystery [that] was made known to [him] by revelation…that is, the gentiles have become fellow heirs, members of the same body, and sharers in the promise in Christ Jesus" (Ephesians 3:3, 6 NRSVue).

The Gospel stories we read during the season of Epiphany are soaked with the surprise and mystery of the revelation of Christ in unexpected places. Living with these stories will remind us that if we become so familiar with the gospel that we fail to be in awe of the love of God revealed in Jesus, it has become far too familiar. Charles Wesley never got over it. His hymns reverberate with the questions like "Amazing love! How can it be?" and "O Love Divine, what hast Thou done?"

And then, joy! The joy the magi experienced when they found the Christ child was not a fizzy happiness that bubbles up for a moment but quickly goes stale and fades away. It was the rich, deep, relentless joy that flows out of the deepest places in the human heart and soul. As we will see at the wedding in Cana, it is joy in the presence of Christ who turns the watery stuff of our ordinary existence into the extraordinary rich wine of the glory of God.

The magi experience the joy of finding at the end of a long and arduous search. Matthew doesn't suggest or explain the backstory for the magi. We know from our own experience that the intensity of our joy is directly proportional to the intensity of our investment in the search for it. Jesus said it's the joy of a shepherd who spent the night searching for a lost sheep, a woman who turned her house upside down searching for a lost coin, and a father who welcomed his lost son home. Each story concludes with a joyful celebration when that which was lost was found (see Luke 15:3-24). One of my mentors described the pattern as "Lost! Found! Party time!"

The magi found joy in the fulfillment of the promise in Deuteronomy: "You will seek the Lord your God from there, and you will find him if you seek him with all your heart and with all your being" (4:29). Jesus repeated that promise in the Sermon on the Mount when he told his disciples, "Ask, and it will be given to you; search, and you will find; knock, and the door will be opened for you. For everyone who asks receives, and everyone who searches finds, and for everyone who knocks, the door will be opened" (Matthew 7:7-8 NRSVue).

Every Epiphany calls for our response. Diana Butler Bass writes, "We may not create epiphanies, but we respond to them. Epiphanies grab a hold of us; we can't shake them. Epiphanies ask something of us. The star is an invitation, a calling to do something—to act."[6] Matthew described the magi "falling to their knees" to honor the child they found, not in a royal palace, but in an ordinary, humble house. "Then they opened their treasure chests and presented him with gifts of gold, frankincense, and myrrh" (Matthew 2:11).

You may have seen the humorous meme of the "wise women" who brought Mary diapers, casseroles, and baby formula. Whatever form the gifts take, they were and are the expression of loving generosity, the model of extravagant gifts of love. It raises the questions: What does it look like for us to give our gifts to the Christ child? How might we do that?

Henry van Dyke imagined one answer to that question in 1895 when he wrote "The Story of The Other Wise Man." I can picture the cover of a well-worn copy of the book in our home when I was growing up. Van Dyke imagined another astrologer named Artaban, who also saw the star and set out to find the newborn king. He brought a sapphire, a ruby, and a pearl. A stop to help a dying man delayed him so that the other magi left without him. He arrived in Bethlehem too late to see the Christ child before his parents fled with him to Egypt. Before leaving Bethlehem, Artaban gave one of his gifts to save the life of another child.

Artaban missed the Holy Family again in Egypt. He kept searching for thirty-three years, giving his gifts to people in need along the way. He ended up in Jerusalem just in time for the crucifixion of the one he had been seeking. He saw Pilate's mocking sign on the cross that identified Jesus as "the King of the Jews." He spent his last treasure, the pearl, on ransom for a young woman who was being sold into slavery. When the earth shook and the sky turned dark, a tile fell from the roof and struck Artaban. He was about to die, convinced that he failed in his quest, when he heard the voice of Jesus saying, "Inasmuch as ye have done it unto one of the least of these my brethren, ye have done it unto me" (Matthew 25:40 KJV). Van Dyke writes, "A calm radiance of wonder and joy lighted the face of Artaban.... His journey was ended. His treasures were accepted. The Other Wise Man found the King."[7]

The guidance of the gospel is that we are most likely to meet the Christ when we give ourselves to others, particularly to people in need. We honor Christ by serving others the way Jesus served; loving others the way Jesus loved.

A well-educated, upwardly mobile young man joined me on a trip to South Africa. His eyes were opened to the remnants of the sinister evil of apartheid. He saw the massive economic inequity and the struggle of people in the shacks of "informal settlements" in the townships. He sat beside the bed of a man who was dying with AIDS. He confessed that he was depressed by what he experienced. But then he watched people who were actively working to offer gifts of healing, hope, and love to others. He served with ordinary people who were doing extraordinary ministry in difficult places. He said that as he looked into their faces, listened to their stories, and felt the passion with which they served, his eyes were opened to the irrepressible joy with which they served and the relentless faith with which they worked for a better day. It was his experience of the Epiphany of Christ. He came back to his community determined to find a way to serve in that spirit at home.

"They departed into their own country another way." (Matthew 2:12 KJV)

I'm sure the recent translations are more accurate in saying the magi went back to their home country "by another route." If they were "wise men," they hardly needed a divine intervention to reset their GPS to find a route home that did not include a return visit to that maniacal con artist in Jerusalem, Herod. Even if it was a longer trip, the odds were better that they would get home alive.

I continue, however, to be intrigued by the phrase in the King James Version, "another way." It suggests more than simply following another highway. Matthew does not give us any information on what happened when they got back home. But I am convinced that because of the Epiphany, they went home by a different way as different people who saw the world differently than they did when their journey began.

They went back to the same old place, but they weren't the same old people. Having seen what they saw, they could never unsee it. It changed the way they saw everything else. Because they caught a glimpse of the glory of God in Christ, they could not be satisfied with the petty bickering, the incessant conflict, the persistent darkness of their old world. Because they experienced a revelation of how the world could be, they could never again settle for the way it is. The magi caught a glimpse of the kingdom of God becoming a reality on earth as it is in heaven. It sent them off on a different journey, living in a different way.

The Epiphany of Christ, however and whenever we experience it, leads us forward as different people living in a different way too.

What the magi found in Bethlehem was not only a destination, but a direction for their journey. The star led them to the One who is "the way, truth and life." The Epiphany for the women at the empty tomb was the good news that "he is going ahead of you into Galilee. You will see him there" (Mark 16:7). The living Christ defines not only the way, the route, or road we follow. Christ also shows us the way to live as we follow his way. Christ becomes the light that always leads us on. John Wesley taught that "the holiest of [people] still need Christ, the light of the world. For he does not give them light, but from moment to moment."[8]

I cannot explain how my GPS works. Nor can I explain the way the Epiphany happens in each of our lives It's a mind-bending, soul-stretching, life-giving mystery to me. I am confident, however, that if we train our eyes to see it, the light of the star that led the magi can find each of us wherever we are and set us on the way to finding the thing we most deeply need and ultimately desire. Like following my GPS, I've learned to trust it. It's become an ordinary part of my life. I wouldn't leave home without it.

OLD EYES AND NEW VISIONS

Luke 2:22-28

I thought I'd be a lot older than I am when I got to be this old. My disturbing epiphany, however, is that I am this old! I will celebrate my seventy-eighth birthday before this book is released. Regardless of how long I'm around, the life ahead of me is a lot shorter than the life behind me. How do we deal with the inevitable limitations and discover the unexpected joys of aging? More specifically, how do we meet Christ in the ordinary experiences of growing older?

A friend I had not seen for three decades surprised me when I was preaching at Lakeside Chautauqua in Ohio. He was the president at the University of Tampa when we moved to the nearby Hyde Park United Methodist Church. He and his wife helped us through some of our most challenging years in ministry with their faithful stability and joyful friendship. They moved to another state, I retired, and we left Tampa. Over the moves and years, we lost touch with each other. He saw I was preaching at Lakeside and showed up on Sunday morning.

We compared notes on our work and retirement over supper. He shared the pain of his wife's battle with cancer and her death on Christmas Eve. As we named the challenges of aging, he broke into a day-brightening smile. With a twinkle in his eye, he said, "Isn't getting older interesting?" The word *interesting* became an epiphany that helped me see the realities of getting older in a different perspective. He looked at aging with curiosity. He was watching for the light of some new epiphany breaking through at any moment along the way.

The twinkle in his eyes reminded me of the eulogy for Moses in Deuteronomy 34:7: "Moses was 120 years old when he died. His eyesight wasn't impaired, and his vigor hadn't diminished a bit." Another translation says Moses died "with eyes undimmed and vigor undiminished" (CJB). Eugene Peterson's paraphrase paints an even livelier portrait: "His eyesight was sharp; he still walked with a spring in his step" (MSG).

Anna and Simeon weren't as old as Moses, but they were heading in that direction (Luke 2:22-38). Luke tells us she was eighty-four. He was no spring chicken either. Over the years I've enjoyed seeing them from a distance, like watching two aging actors who bring their personal maturity into their characters on the stage or screen. I remember Henry Fonda and Katharine Hepburn in *On Golden Pond*, Will Geer and Ellen Corby as Grandpa and Grandma on *The Waltons*, or Maggie Smith's acerbic accuracy as the Dowager Countess of Grantham on *Downton Abbey*.

I've watched Anna and Simeon from the outside as if I were sitting in the balcony, but that view is changing. Give or take a few years, I'll catch up with them. I've begun seeing these fascinating characters from the inside out, as if I were the actor on the stage. I'm discovering the way their story helps me be prepared to experience the Epiphany in my life right now.

> ## "In accordance with the Law from Moses, they brought Jesus up to Jerusalem to present him to the Lord." (Luke 2:22)

It must have been an ordinary day in the Temple. Luke doesn't indicate that it was one of the "High Holy Days" or one of the great festivals that brought the huge crowds to Jerusalem. There was nothing unusual about faithful Jewish parents bringing their firstborn male children for the dedication forty days after their birth. It was part of the biblical law handed down from Moses (Exodus 13:2).

There was nothing extraordinary about Simeon and Anna being in the temple that day. Luke describes Simeon as "righteous and devout." He "eagerly anticipated the restoration of Israel, and the Holy Spirit rested on him." He lived for many years with the promise that he would not die before he saw the Christ (Luke 2:25-27). Luke's Gospel gives special attention to the women in the story from Elizabeth in the beginning to the women at the tomb at the end. He identifies Anna as a "prophet" who "never left the temple but worshipped God [there] with fasting and prayer night and day." Like Simeon, she was "looking forward to the redemption of Jerusalem" (Luke 2:37-38).

Anna and Simeon were like the aging, longtime members of the little church I served in rural Florida. They were there every time the door opened. In fact, Edna Mae and Elizabeth along with her husband, Don, were usually the ones who opened the doors. They were the first folks to show up when I, as a freshly minted, liturgically trained seminary graduate, announced that we would begin Advent by "hanging the greens." I can hear their deep, Southern laughter when they asked if I intended to hang collards or turnip greens. They were laughing, but like Anna and Simeon, they were always there. They went on to heaven years ago, but I can't imagine that congregation without them.

But something extraordinary happened on that otherwise normal day. Simeon's aging eyes caught a glimpse of a particular child in the arms of two otherwise ordinary parents. Simeon took the child in his arthritic, old arms and, like the opening scene in *The Lion King*, he lifted the child up, praising God for the fulfillment of the promise. His words became embedded in the liturgical tradition as the *Nunc Dimittis*, meaning "now let us depart."

> *Now, master, let your servant go in peace according to your word,*
>   *because my eyes have seen your salvation.*
> *You prepared this salvation in the presence of all peoples.*
> *It's a light for revelation to the Gentiles*
>   *and a glory for your people Israel.*
>
> (Luke 2:29-32)

It must be an understatement for Luke to say Mary and Joseph were "amazed." They never expected this. They were simply doing what the law required. Simeon's reaction added another surprise to all the amazing things they had already experienced—experiences Mary stored away in her heart. The unnerving surprise, however, came when Simeon looked deeply into Mary's eyes and predicted:

> *This boy is assigned to be the cause of the falling and rising of many in Israel and to be a sign that generates opposition so that the inner thoughts of many will be revealed. And a sword will pierce your innermost being too.*
>
> (Luke 2:34-35)

Simeon's ominous words must have left everyone speechless. Luke doesn't describe Simeon's response to the revelation of the glory of God in the Christ child or his dark forecast of what was ahead. He saw the vision he had been promised. That was enough. Did he die with joyful gratitude for the fulfillment of the promise or with pain-soaked tears because of his foreboding vision of the future? Or was it both? Luke left no doubt about Anna's response. She immediately became the cheerleader for a long-predicted but now-realized future. She ran off as quickly as her rickety old legs could carry her to point out this child to "everyone who was looking forward to the redemption of Jerusalem" (Luke 2:38).

So, how does the story of these aging saints invite us to experience the Epiphany as we get older? What did they learn across the years of their lives that might prepare us to meet Christ in the ordinary process of aging?

"Guided by the Spirit, Simeon came into the temple." (Luke 2:27 NRSVue)

Simeon and Anna learned to listen deeply for the guidance of the Spirit. Their years of devotion and worship trained all their senses to be alive and awake for the Spirit to lead them to the right place at the right time to experience the Epiphany of Christ.

As I came down from the balcony and stepped onto the stage with Anna and Simeon, I found myself humming the African American spiritual "Every Time I Feel the Spirit." Matthew Brady caught a photograph of a group of escaped slaves singing that song when Abraham Lincoln visited a "contraband" camp on Seventh Street in Washington, DC. According to some versions of the story, Lincoln joined in the singing.[1]

The Spirit-filled listening Lincoln experienced with the slaves didn't drop in from nowhere. It emerged from a deep, inner openness to experience the presence of the Spirit moving in their hearts and souls. Their faithful listening was rooted in the words and stories of Scripture handed down orally from generation to generation the way Alex Haley described the process in *Roots: The Saga of an American Family*. Their faith was sustained over the long haul by songs that became the inner rhythms of their souls to express abounding joy, soul-wrenching sorrow, conspiratorial faith, and courageous hope.

Listening did not come naturally for me. My forbears were German and Irish immigrants. Folks in my family have strong opinions, and we're ready to fight for them! We are all grateful for my Italian uncle, who said he married into our family to improve the bloodline. I am a talker who grew up in a family of talkers. I have childhood memories of my father and uncles arguing in the living room while their wives were in the kitchen and the kids were playing upstairs. I remember Aunt Eleanor shaking her head as she said, "They're at it again." She would finally step into the living room to tell them it was time to go home.

My major in college was in speech and drama, and I honed my speaking skills as a member of the debate team. My sense of calling to be a preacher may have had something to do with telling people the truth I thought and believed they needed to hear. I grew up among people who believed deeply in prayer, but my understanding of prayer largely focused on talking to God, telling God what I wanted to say, rather than listening in silence for the Spirit to speak to me.

My formative experience of prayerful silence occurred during seminary when our church history professor, Kenneth Cain Kinghorn, invited a small group of students to spend a night at the Abbey of Gethsemani. Located in the peaceful, rolling hills of western Kentucky, it was the monastic home of Thomas Merton. A silent beauty permeated the place. We watched from the balcony as the monks quietly entered the sanctuary and found their way to their stalls. They opened their books and waited in silence for the bell to ring. Then they chanted the psalms, listened to the scripture, and waited in silence. There would be time for talking over their work or in their chapter gatherings where they had recently debated bringing in a television to see Neil Armstrong take his first steps on the surface of the moon, but their community was bound together in silence.

I am not called to a monastic life of silence, but I'm grateful for the monks who are still there, still listening in prayerful silence. I often return to Gethsemani in memory to center myself in prayerful listening. E. Stanley Jones called his daily time of prayer "the listening post" where he would get his "marching orders" for the day. More times than I can count, the words in my prayer journey are "Lord, quiet the noisy voices in my brain, calm my anxious energy, meet me in the silence, and guide me into this day with the presence of your Spirit."

As I paid attention to Simeon from the inside out, I asked some probing questions about him that quickly became questions I ask myself.

What if Simeon slept in that day?

What if he skipped his "listening post" that morning?

What if he felt the Spirit moving in his heart but didn't feel like responding to it?

What if he decided to sit on the porch with another cup of coffee or watch his favorite morning news show rather than be in his regular place in the temple when parents came with their children?

What if he missed the Epiphany of the Christ because he wasn't listening for the Spirit?

What if I sometimes miss the Epiphany because of my answers to those questions?

Elise Ballard became a secular authority on epiphanies through her research, books, videos, and TED Talks. She found that people have epiphanies "because they are ready for them." She encourages us to "cultivate an environment in our lives and within ourselves so that we're always ready and open for epiphanies.... We want to live in tune with our inner voice and wisdom so that epiphanies come easily, and we get the message."[2] By practicing the spiritual disciplines of their tradition, Simeon and Anna cultivated the environment that prepared them to experience the Epiphany.

"[Simeon] was righteous and devout, looking forward to the consolation of Israel." (Luke 2:25 NRSVue)

Simeon and Anna learned to wait in hope. The writer of Psalm 130 described the way they had been hoping and waiting year after long year for something they might not live long enough to see.

> My whole being hopes,
> and I wait for God's promise.
> My whole being waits for my Lord—

> more than the night watch waits for morning;
> yes, more than the night watch waits for morning!
> (Psalm 130:5-6)

Anna and Simeon stand in the long line of Old Testament characters who waited in hope. They lived in the "in-between space" between the already and the not yet, between the way the world is and the prophetic promise of what will come. Followers of Christ in every generation live between the kingdom of God revealed in Jesus and the hope of the day when God's kingdom will come and God's will is done on earth as it is in heaven. In the interim, we wait in hope.

The summer of 1943 found Dietrich Bonhoeffer in prison. He was waiting to go on trial for his participation in a plot to assassinate Hitler. His nephew, Christoph von Dohnányi, wrote a letter in which he expressed his hope for the day the family would be reunited. "Hopefully, it will happen. Then the family will be back together again.... And then the long-awaited celebration will come. One must just wait patiently. Sometime that day will come for certain."[3]

The following day, Bonhoeffer expressed the same hope in a letter to his parents. He said the gifts they sent "draw my thoughts daily toward that day we are already all looking forward to.... I can't contribute anything here toward it except wait and anticipate it with joy."[4]

It's hard to wait! Our short-attention-span culture conditions us to expect anything and everything to happen immediately. Amazon.com is a gigantic business success not only because they have just about anything we want but because they deliver it so quickly. A forceful voice within us is constantly commanding our attention by shouting, "Don't just sit there! Do something!" But hopeful waiting is not doing nothing. Waiting in hope means living now in ways that are consistent with the way we believe things will be when "the kingdom of the world has become the kingdom of our Lord and his Christ" (Revelation 11:15). Waiting in hope means acting now as if the future is already here, knowing that it is here in us. How do we practice that kind of active waiting when things don't go the way we hoped?

The day after the 2024 presidential election, a faithful man who is at least a decade younger than I am asked if we could meet for coffee. My friend brought two pages of typewritten observations and questions, concluding with, "Where do we go from here? What gives you hope?"

As we talked, I reminded my friend and myself that as people of biblical faith, we've been here before. The biblical writers never hid the stories of kings, leaders, and ordinary people who failed to live up to God's vision or who rejected God's way. Everything that happens is not necessarily God's will. In a democracy, God doesn't select the president; the people do. But through it all, God continues to be relentlessly at work to accomplish God's redemptive purpose in the messy and mangled realities of human history. As followers of Christ, we are called to be the living presence of the kingdom of God regardless of who resides in the White House. I shared four options for hopeful waiting.

We can rest and breathe.

Diana Butler Bass offered helpful advice during the night as the results came in. "Go slow tomorrow. I urge you to pay attention to some small, beautiful things in your life. We don't need answers or a plan or even understanding right now. One friend did text me, 'It's okay to need to catch your breath after the wind has been knocked out. It will take a bit. But we will rise.'"[5]

Waiting in hope is a long-term deal. It requires us to hold onto our vision of the future even when we face defeats along the way; even when decades of progress toward the promise of the "beloved community" and "a more perfect union" are blocked or delayed. To sustain our faith, we must learn the balance of action and silence, work and rest, laughter and tears. As we get older, we learn what British poet T. S. Eliot had in mind when he prayed these words:

> Teach us to care and not to care.
> Teach us to sit still.[6]

We can weep.

There is more than ample biblical support for weeping. Nearly half of the psalms are psalms of lament. Old Testament prophets like Jeremiah and Hosea wept over the direction their nation had taken. Jesus wept because the city of Jerusalem could not see the way of peace. When hopes are defeated or delayed, it's appropriate to weep over the loss of what we believe might have been.

We can listen.

We can listen to one another as we work through our disappointments and confusion. The fact that the results were so profoundly different than we expected may mean that we had not listened deeply enough to the frustrations, grievances, and fears of people around us. We can listen to the witness of faithful people who have gone through similar experiences in the past. And we can listen more deeply for the voice of the Spirit to speak to us and give us a fresh sense of direction for the future.

We can go on doing what we are called to do in the places we are called to do it.

A friend of mine is a pediatrician and associate chief medical officer of a major hospital. She is also a person of deep faith. On the morning after the 2024 presidential election, she wrote a message to her staff:

> I have been asked this morning what we do now. What we do is we get up, we go to work, we continue to fight for the rights of all people,

the protections of children, the idea of democracy. We get up, we go to work, we hug our families, we love our children, we pray for our country, we believe in God, and we stand for what is good and right and we use data, facts and science to advocate for children.[7]

Waiting in hope calls us to go forward, stumbling and limping toward the vision of God's kingdom coming on earth as it is in heaven. We keep living in ways that are consistent with the way revealed in the words, way, and will of Jesus Christ.

Yolanda Pierce, the dean of the Vanderbilt Divinity School, affirmed, "Waiting on God is an active process...perhaps God is waiting on me....Maybe the between time is about not just God's work but also my own: the work that I must do to be ready to receive the instructions, the next assignment, the blessing, or the answers."[8]

My friend and his wife practiced that active faith on the morning after the election. They made baked goods and delivered them to their friends who supported the opposing side. He wrote, "We know they know we are disappointed, but they know we always help them and show kindness." Their small act of kindness reminded me of words from a hymn I grew up singing in worship.

> For not with swords' loud clashing
> or roll of stirring drums
> with deeds of love and mercy
> the heavenly kingdom comes.[9]

Simeon and Anna learned to honor the past while looking toward the future. Their lives were soaked in the words of the prophets and the hopes of Israel from which they looked to the future.

One of my mentors during my early years in ministry was O. Dean Martin. He was the pastor of Trinity United Methodist Church in Gainesville and the chaplain of the University of Florida football team. Dean told the story of a friend who lost his job in one of those brutal, bureaucratic shuffles that happen with painful regularity in the business world. Dean called his friend to see how he was doing during his last day on the job. His friend replied, "I'm okay. I figure there's a lot more glass in the windshield than there is in the rear-view mirror. I'm not looking back. I'm looking ahead."

Dean's friend was not, of course, the first person to use that metaphor, but it was the first time I heard it. It stuck with me because the observation is obvious. There is, in fact, more glass in the windshield than the rear-view mirror. The reason is just as obvious. When we're driving down the highway, it's more important to see where we are going than where we have been.

Rear-view are mirrors so important they are required by law. If we don't understand where we've been and how we got to where we are, we won't have a clue about how to get to where we're going. To live without honoring our past is like cutting branches off from the trunk of the tree. But it's critically important to keep our eyes on the road ahead. The windshield metaphor takes us back to the eulogy of Moses.

It's a poignant scene. Moses is alone on Mount Pisgah looking out across the hills and valleys toward the Promised Land, just the way folks look out across the Great Smoky Mountains and the Pisgah National Forest in North Carolina. In the rear-view mirror we see the amazing story of the way God brought the Hebrew people out of slavery in Egypt, guided them through the wilderness, gave them the Law, and sustained them on the long journey toward the Promised Land. The writer of Deuteronomy brings Moses's story to completion by saying, "His sight was unimpaired, and his vigor had not abated" (Deuteronomy 34:7 NRSVue). Fully aware of everything in the past, Moses died with his eyes fixed on the future.

Aging can merely be the inevitable process of getting older, or it can be the intentional process of getting better. It depends on the direction we are looking. People who have seen the revelation of the glory of God in Christ can't unsee it. Their eyes are fixed on a hope-filled vision of the future. People like Martin Luther King Jr., Nelson Mandela, Ruth Bader Ginsburg, and John Lewis lived with divine dissatisfaction about the way things are because they caught a glimpse of the way things can and will ultimately be. Having seen the kingdom of God in the words and way of Jesus, his disciples want to actively participate in that kingdom right here, right now. Because they believe the arc of the moral universe bends toward justice, they want to put their weight on the side doing the bending. They know why windshields are larger than rearview mirrors.

As a pastor I've known many people who were older than I am now, though I'm rapidly catching up with them! Sadly, I've known people whose eyes were fixed on the past. They could not get over what they had seen or done or what the world had done to them. Their vision was clouded by grievance, disappointment, defeat, or despair. They could neither accept change in the present nor anticipate hope for the future. They longed to return to some mythical glory day that may or may not have been as great as they believed. Instead of becoming better, they became bitter and brittle.

By contrast, I've been blessed to know many faithful people like Anna and Simeon. As they became older, they became better. They validated words from Dag Hammarskjöld that appeared on a poster on my college dorm room wall: "If only I may grow: firmer, simpler—quieter, warmer."[10] They never forgot or rejected their past, but they grew deeper, stronger, more loving, and more joyful as they looked toward the future.

We were preparing to launch the first phase of the master plan that became a nine-year project to renovate the existing buildings and construct new ones on the property of Hyde Park United Methodist Church. I visited one of the "elder statesmen" of the congregation to ask if he would chair the first financial campaign. He turned me down, not because he didn't believe in the project, but because he wanted to encourage and support a new generation of leaders. He offered me wisdom borne out of his long history in the congregation when he said, "Do it for the children! Focus your attention on them. We all have children and grandchildren. This church is here for them, not just for us." Other aging church members whose eyes were undimmed kept saying, "Let's get on with this. I want to see it completed before I die!"

I've been one of the retired members of our annual conference for more than a decade. Francis Asbury, the first bishop of Methodism in America, referred to us as "worn out preachers." Sitting in the balcony, we could be like Statler and Waldorf, the cantankerous old guys on *The Muppet Show* who heckled the cast on the stage from their box seats. We might be tempted to look down on the congregations we served and wonder why they aren't doing things the way we did them. The alternative is to be the cheerleaders for the future whose primary role is to encourage young leaders who will guide the church, community, and nation into an unpredictable future.

As a facilitator for the Institute of Preaching, I am engaged with some of the young, fresh pastors who are coming into our conference. I am amazed by the depth of their commitment and the hopeful passion they bring to ministry in a church and culture that are radically different from the era in which I entered ministry. Working with them, I remember words my senior pastor spoke to me as a young minister when I confronted some new problem or challenge. He would lean back in his chair and say, "I can't wait to see how you work this one out!"

Luke brings down the curtain on this act of the Epiphany drama with words that set the stage for the future.

> When Mary and Joseph had completed everything required by the Law of the Lord, they returned to their hometown, Nazareth in Galilee. The child grew up and became strong. He was filled with wisdom, and God's favor was on him.
>
> (Luke 2:39-40)

Anna and Simeon take their final bow. They leave the stage, and we never see them again. They would not live long enough to see what became of the child they celebrated in the temple that day. It was enough for them to see with their own eyes the revelation of God's glory in the face of the infant Jesus. They bore witness to what they had seen. They played their part in the drama of the kingdom of God coming on earth and that was enough.

There is still room on the stage for aging witnesses who point others to the love of God revealed in Christ. The same Spirit who was at work through Anna and Simeon can use our experience from the past to point toward the future. Following their example certainly makes life more interesting!

I close this chapter with a word of encouragement for my aging generation from a previous one, namely, the nineteenth-century British poet Alfred, Lord Tennyson, in "Ulysses."

> Come, my friends,
> 'Tis not too late to seek a newer world.
> . . . .
> Though much is taken, much abides; and though
> We are not now that strength which in old days
> Moved earth and heaven, that which we are, we are,
> One equal temper of heroic hearts,
> Made weak by time and fate, but strong in will
> To strive, to seek, to find, and not to yield.

MEETING CHRIST IN DARK PLACES

Matthew 2:16-23

Imagine a first-century twenty-four-hour cable news channel in Jerusalem interrupting the talk-show chatter to deliver the breaking news headline "Herod Orders Slaughter of Boys in Bethlehem." The story continues:

> We just received reports from Bethlehem that King Herod's troops are obeying the command to murder every boy two years of age or younger. Parents are attempting to escape, some migrating illegally across the border into Egypt. Among them are the parents of the child who may have caused the massacre. Astrologers who arrived in Jerusalem recently located a boy in Bethlehem whom they assumed to be the newborn king. Herod ordered them to report back to him when they found the child. According to anonymous sources in the palace, the king flew into a rage when he realized the astrologers tricked him by returning to their home country by a different route.

Our imaginary reporter catches her breath and holds back tears. It is reminiscent of the moment Walter Cronkite paused, took off his glasses, and nearly wept when he announced that President Kennedy was dead or when Tom Brokaw reported the fall of the Twin Towers on 9/11. She gathers her emotions and continues.

"Reports sweeping across the village remind observant Jews of the words of the prophet Jeremiah:

> *A voice [was] heard in Ramah,*
> *weeping and wailing,*
> *It's Rachel crying for her children;*
> *she [refused] to be consoled,*
> *because her children are no more.*
> *(Jeremiah 31:15)*

"Our cameras are on the way to Bethlehem. We will have video at eleven, but we warn you that the images will be disturbing. That's all for now."

What's this horrendous story doing in Matthew's Gospel? The other Gospel writers either did not have this story or left it out. After all, the word *gospel* means "good news." So, where's the good news in a story like this? If Epiphany is the revelation of the glory of God in Jesus Christ, where's the glory in the tears of the grieving parents in Bethlehem?

If we have problems with this story, we aren't alone. Scholars find no external record for the massacre in Bethlehem. I suppose it's possible that Herod's sycophantic followers rewrote history to bury this gruesome event. It's also possible that Matthew included the story for a theological rather than a historical purpose. Some scholars see it as the affirmation that God saved the infant Jesus from Herod's wrath the way the infant Moses escaped Pharaoh's slaughter of the Hebrew boys. It places Jesus in the tradition of the Old Testament from the very beginning of his life.

As a former tax collector, Matthew took part in a corrupt political and economic system that took advantage of the Hebrew community for the sake of wealth and the power of the Roman Empire. He knew the machinations of political power. This Gospel reveals the persistent tension between the kingdoms of this world, ruled by the likes of Herod at the beginning of Jesus's life and Pilate at its end, versus the kingdom of God revealed in Jesus. Matthew's collection of Jesus's teachings in the Sermon on the Mount is nothing short of an underground manual for a community that becomes a radical alternative to the assumed values and actions of the empire in every age.

With or without an external record, historians agree the massacre in Bethlehem sounds like something Herod might do. He was a pathological narcissist who was obsessively driven by his fear of any threat to his position or anything that might undermine his power in the Roman Empire. Along with killing his enemies, he had no qualms about killing family members and former friends as well.

Herod had been crowned "King of the Jews" by the Roman Senate in 40 BC in Rome. The magi's search for the newly born "King of the Jews" sets in motion the deadly conflict that reaches its climax in Jesus's conversation with Pilate (Matthew 18:28–19:16). The Roman governor condemned Jesus to death for political, not religious, reasons when the crowd reminded him, "If you release this man, you are no friend of the emperor. Everyone who claims to be a king sets himself against the emperor" (John 19:12 NRSVue). His decision is consistent with the decisions of political operatives in every authoritarian empire. Pilate posted the mocking notice "Jesus of Nazareth, the King of the Jews" on the cross (John 19:20 JBP). It was a direct warning to any other subversive movement, the ultimate declaration of the power of the empire over the apparent weakness of the kingdom of God.

The brutal story of the massacre in Bethlehem is disturbingly consistent with the "Breaking News" in our own time. From Gaza to Ukraine to the hallways of elementary schools in the United States, we see the reports of children's deaths in a world of warfare and gun violence.

The unsettling truth is that much of our world is still Herod's world. The story of the massacre in Bethlehem is our story. We are tempted to turn away from the headlines to hide away in a comfortable cocoon of a personal piety that focuses on finding our "best life" or on getting ready to go to heaven. We try to close our eyes to the injustice and suffering around us along with our unintentional participation in it until some undesired epiphany forces us to see what we would prefer not to see.

"A sword will pierce your innermost being too." (Luke 2:35)

Along with the "macro" stories of massive suffering and pain in our world, we confront the "micro" stories in individual lives. They are deeply intimate and profoundly personal stories that pierce our hearts the way Simeon predicted would happen for Mary (Luke 2:35). Eventually, every one of us will weep with the brokenhearted parents in Bethlehem when we experience the inevitable pain in our own lives or the lives of people we love, often inflicted upon us by forces we cannot control.

I believe Matthew's Gospel included the Bethlehem massacre as a bold declaration that the Epiphany includes the revelation of the extraordinary presence of Christ in the ordinary places of human suffering, grief, injustice, and pain. Perhaps the early church preserved this ghastly account to affirm that the glory of God in Christ is uncovered unexpectedly beneath, behind, and within the darkness of our pain and loss.

"Jesus wept" (John 11:35 KJV) is the shortest verse in the Bible. It is also a powerful expression of the flesh-and-blood reality of the Incarnation. If Jesus is Emmanuel, meaning "God with us," he is with us when we walk through the dark "valley of the shadow of death" as surely as he is with us when we "lie down in green pastures" and rest "beside the still waters" (Psalm 23:2, 4 KJV). When Jesus wept over Jerusalem; when he wept beside the grave of Lazarus; when he wept in the garden of Gethsemane; and when he cried, "My God, why?" from the cross, his cries echoed the weeping of the parents in Bethlehem in every generation. From the earliest days of his life to his final breath, Jesus was real human flesh—really with us in our very real grief and pain.

I tread carefully around this story because I have not faced the incomparable pain of the death of my children or grandchildren. But as a pastor, I've had the sacred privilege of being with parents who lost a child. I remember the faces of parents who watched their early elementary-school-age daughter die in her mother's arms because of a degenerative disease. I rode with them to the hospital and held back my own tears as the nurse gently received the lifeless body into her arms. I was with more than one set of parents who lost their child in a car accident. I stood with a mother as her adult son with cancer took his last breath. I read the words of committal as parents whose adult son took his own life laid his ashes to rest in the church's memorial garden. I remember their names, hear their weeping, and carry with me a small part of their pain.

My wife and I shared the long journey with close friends whose son died because of alcohol addiction. They wrote the obituary that named the grief we all felt. "Matthew died too early. Way too early. Everybody loved Matthew…everybody." With painful honesty, they described the soul-searing truth:

> The last few years of Matthew's life were marred by the disease of alcohol addiction. He was working on getting his life back through both inpatient and outpatient treatment programs, AA, and personal counseling. The road to recovery is long and hard with many stumbles along the way. Matthew was on that road when he had his final stumble on April 9, 2024.

The clarity of their words reminded me of Shakespeare's closing lines in *King Lear*:

> The weight of this sad time we must obey,
> Speak what we feel and not what we ought to say.[1]

The easy thing for any of us to do in "this sad time" is fall back on the pleasant platitudes we think we ought to say. The hard thing is to speak the truth of what we most deeply feel. Matthew's pastor, friend, and spiritual counselor spoke the truth in the memorial service. Drawing on Psalm 23, he named the darkness of walking through the "valley of the shadow of death." But he also named the promise that "goodness and mercy shall follow me all the days of my life: and I will dwell in the house of the LORD for ever" (Psalm 23:6 KJV). He affirmed the assurance Paul announced to the Romans, "Nothing can separate us from God's love in Christ" (see Romans 8:38).

I believe every word Matthew's pastor shared. I believe that nothing can separate us from the love of God. But if I speak the truth about what we feel in times like this, I am forced to say that, for now, we feel the frustration and pain of loss. Matthew and the people who loved him did everything they could to save him. We prayed to the God who loved Matthew before he was born; the God who gave Matthew life and claimed him as God's child at his baptism; the God to whom Matthew committed himself in confirmation; the God to whom Matthew prayed; the God whose essential character revealed in his Son is love that never lets us go. We prayed for Matthew to win the fight with alcoholism and go on living the life for which God had created him. But alcoholism won. Matthew lost. Everyone who loved him lost. We are tempted to feel that God lost too.

To suggest that "God lost" pushes against the grain of what we think we ought to say and what we want to say. But if we speak what we *feel*, we find ourselves in the company of the writers of the psalms of lament.

Old Testament scholar Ellen Davis says these "cries of anguish and rage would seem to violate all the rules for Christian prayer.... These prayers are not polite."[2] The psalmists invite us to name with brutal honesty our sense of the *Deus absconditus*, the "hidden God." With Jesus on the cross, we identify with the psalmist who cried,

> *My God! My God,*
> > *why have you left me all alone?*
> > *Why are you so far from saving me—*
> > > *so far from my anguished groans?*
> *My God, I cry out during the day,*
> > *but you don't answer;*
> > *even at nighttime I don't stop.*
> > > (Psalm 22:1-2)

The amazing thing about these psalms is that the darkest cries of loss, frustration, fear, and anger are expressed in prayer to the God they feel has forgotten them. "Almost invariably, the psalmist comes out in a different place than she first entered into prayer.... [These psalmists] move fitfully in the direction of praise."[3] The psalm Jesus quoted on the cross moves toward these words of assurance:

> *I will declare your name to my brothers and sisters;*
> > *I will praise you in the very center of the congregation!*
> *All of you who revere the* LORD—*praise him!*
> > *All of you who are Jacob's descendants—honor him!*
> > *All of you who are all Israel's offspring—*
> > > *stand in awe of him!*
> *Because he didn't despise or detest*
> > *the suffering of the one who suffered—*
> > *he didn't hide his face from me.*
> > *No, he listened when I cried out to him for help.*
> > > (Psalm 22:22-24)

I've come to believe the voice within us that shouts "No! This isn't the way it's supposed to be!" is nothing less than the Spirit of God praying within us with groans too deep for words (Romans 8:26-27). As I've wrestled biblically with so many deaths like Matthew's, I've come to a clear conviction.

If God's desire is abundant life for all his children (John 10:10)...

If death is the "last enemy" to be destroyed (1 Corinthians 15:26-28)...

If the relentless love of God is the power that will ultimately triumph over every power of evil, sin, pain, and death (Revelation 21:1-6)...

And if prayer is joining God's Spirit groaning within us in hope of a yet-to-be-healed creation (Romans 8:18-39)...

When forces we cannot control take the life of one of God's children, God's perfect will for life is in that moment defeated, as surely as God's love made flesh in Jesus was defeated at the cross. For the time being, we feel as if we live in the silent shadows of Holy Saturday, holding onto the aching hope of resurrection. Matthew's parents concluded the obituary with a deep expression of hope-filled assurance:

> Matthew loved God. And God loves him. Everybody loves Matthew—especially God. Because of Matthew's love for God, and God's unstoppable love for him, we commend him into God's care as he begins the never-ending adventure of eternity, "in which every chapter is better than the one before" and the story never ends. But we miss him. He died too early. Way too early.

Two things are true at the same time. Biblical faith always holds us in the tension of the "already" and the "not yet." We live with the jarring defeat of evil, injustice, and death. At the same time, we live with relentless confidence that God will ultimately win the victory. Ellen Davis affirmed "the fundamental article of biblical religion, namely, that God's life, God's glory, even God's well-being, are indissolubly linked with our lives....Ultimately God must triumph over human death."[4] Paul declared, "Death is the last enemy to be brought to an end" (1 Corinthians 15:26). We commit our loved ones to the grave in the assurance that "if the Spirit of the one who raised Jesus from the dead lives in you, the one who raised Christ from the dead will give life to your human bodies also, through his Spirit that lives in you" (Romans 8:11).

I first heard William Sloane Coffin preach at the Riverside Church in New York City in 1975 and received his sermons by mail every week that followed until his retirement. The sermon he preached on the Sunday after his son's death in 1983 became a formative word for my faith and ministry. It's a classic sermon for people facing this kind of loss. I've quoted it in books and sermons and have offered copies of it to more people than I can count.

Coffin began with the heartbreaking news: "A week ago last Monday night, driving in a terrible storm, my son Alexander, who enjoyed beating his old man at every game and in every race, beat his father to the grave." Responding to the person who suggested that Alex's death was somehow God's will, Coffin declared, "Nothing so infuriates me as the incapacity of seemingly intelligent people to get it through their heads that God doesn't go around the world with his finger on triggers, his fist around knives, his hands on steering wheels.... My own consolation lies in knowing that it was not the will of God that Alex die; that when the waves closed over the sinking car, God's heart was the first of all our hearts to break."

Coffin concluded with a bold affirmation: "I know that when Alex beat me to the grave, the finish line was not Boston Harbor in the middle of the night. If a week ago last Monday, a lamp went out, it was because, for him at least, the Dawn had come."[5] In a few words, a grieving father in New York City could have been offering a word of honest faith and relentless hope to the grieving parents in Bethlehem.

"After King Herod died..." (Matthew 2:19)

Within a few years, the same Jerusalem news anchor who reported the Bethlehem massacre announced the breaking news: "King Herod Is Dead! Reliable sources indicate he died after an unidentified but excruciatingly painful, horrible illness." For Matthew's account in the Gospel, the reports brought a hopeful conclusion to a gruesome story.

Herod had his day. He did his worst. Like Macbeth, he strutted and fretted his hour upon the stage and then was heard no more. He inflicted suffering, pain, and death on innocent people. But when Herod was gone, Jesus came back. "Joseph got up, took the child and his mother, and went to the land of Israel" (Matthew 2:21). Even Herod could not defeat the love of God that became flesh in Jesus. It was a precursor of the end of Matthew's Gospel when Pilate commanded the guards at the tomb, "Make it as secure as you can" (Matthew 27:65 NRSVue). But after the Sabbath, in spite of the power and authority of the Roman Empire, the tomb broke open and the risen Christ came back. The white-robed angel told the women, "Don't be afraid...'He's been raised from the dead. He's going on ahead of you to Galilee. You will see him there'" (Matthew 28:5-7).

The promise at the empty tomb is a hopeful word for all who face the dark, Herod-like realities of our world. Evil will have its day. We will share the genuine hurt and suffering of its power. The darkness is real, but it is not permanent. The risen Christ has been released from the darkness of the tomb and goes before us. The Epiphany still happens, even there!

In the darkest days of the struggle for civil rights in the United States, Martin Luther King Jr. often reminded his followers, "The moral arc of the universe is long, but it bends toward justice." Injustice, suffering, pain, and death are real, but they are not permanent. We live toward the day when "night will be no more. They won't need the light of a lamp or the light of the sun, for the Lord God will shine on them, and they will rule forever" (Revelation 22:5).

Meanwhile, the writer of the Epistle to the Hebrews named the truth we know but hesitate to acknowledge. "As it is, we do not yet see everything in subjection to God's will, but we see Jesus who for a little while was made lower than the angels, now crowned with glory and honor because of the suffering of death, so that by the grace of God he might taste death for everyone" (Hebrews 2:8-9 author's paraphrase).

As things are, we don't see all things under the rule of God's perfect will for us or for the creation. Not everything that happens in this world is consistent with the will and purpose of God. The power of evil sometimes contradicts the way of Christ and inflicts suffering upon us, our world, and the whole creation. But we still see Jesus. The Epiphany of Christ assures us that one who shared our flesh and blood, birth to earth, womb to tomb, can help all who suffer and intends to bring us to glory.

I cannot promise that Herod will not have his day in our lives. But I can promise that Herod's reign will ultimately end and Christ will reign forever.

I cannot promise that faith in Christ will provide immunity from the pain and suffering of this world, and I don't believe the preachers who promise that it can. But I can promise that Christ goes with us through all suffering to bring us with him to new life.

I cannot promise that you will never walk through the darkness in the "valley of the shadow of death." But I can promise that there is a light that shines in the darkness, and the darkness will never be able to put it out (John 1:5).

So, where is the Epiphany of Christ in the dark shadows of the slaughter in Bethlehem? Matthew wants us to know that Christ is present with us in the realities of suffering, injustice, pain, and death. It may, in fact, be through the dark shadows of pain that we find God.

While writing this chapter I've been remembering the stories of people I have known who came face-to-face with the powers of injustice, evil, pain, and death. When they speak what they feel, not what others have told them they ought to say, they often sound like the Old Testament story of Job. Put aside simplistic chatter about "the patience of Job." After all he has gone through, Job is anything but patient. He vigorously argues his case and is ruthlessly honest in naming his grief, frustration, and his sense of the absence of God.

> *Oh, that I could know how to find him—*
> *come to his dwelling place...*
> *Look, I go east; he's not there,*
> *west, and don't discover him;*
> *north in his activity, and I don't grasp him;*
> *he turns south, and I don't see...*
> *he has hidden deep darkness from me.*
> *(Job 23:3, 8-9, 17)*

But the day comes when Job tells the Lord, "I had heard of you by the hearing of the ear, / but now my eye sees you" (Job 42:5 NRSVue). His epiphany of God's presence came through what he suffered, not despite it. He is given new eyes to see himself and the world around him in the larger vision of the creative power and everlasting goodness of God.

Dietrich Bonhoeffer described a similar epiphany in the prologue to his *Letters and Papers from Prison*. He wrote:

> It remains an experience of incomparable value that we have for once learned to see the great events of world history from below, from the perspective of the outcast, the suspect, the maltreated, the powerless, the oppressed and reviled, in short from the perspective of the suffering.... We have come to see matters great and small, happiness and misfortune, strength and weakness with new eyes.[6]

Meeting Christ in Dark Places

Frank Mason North experienced the Epiphany on the crowded streets of New York City during the era Mark Twain dubbed the Gilded Age. The late nineteenth century was a time of economic expansion, materialistic grandeur, and excess in the United States. It was also an era of widespread poverty, inequality, and political corruption. As millions of immigrants, including my forebears, poured into the United States, wealth and political influence were concentrated in the hands of the few who amassed vast fortunes, largely oblivious to the suffering of the forgotten lower classes.

North was ordained in The Methodist Episcopal Church in 1872. He became a leader in the social gospel movement, which engaged him in the massive amount of poverty and suffering beneath the gilded veneer of New York City society. The visual imagery in his hymn describes the setting in which he experienced the Epiphany of Christ:

> Where cross the crowded ways of life,
> where sound the cries of race and clan,
> above the noise of selfish strife,
> we hear your voice, O Son of man.
> In haunts of wretchedness and need,
> on shadowed thresholds dark with fears,
> from paths where hide the lures of greed,
> we catch the vision of your tears.

No imaginary twenty-four-hour cable news reporter interrupted the daily talk shows to deliver the "breaking news" when Frank Mason North met Christ on the busy streets and in the shadowed slums of nineteenth-century New York City. It was a quiet Epiphany, unnoticed in nightmare of a dark and suffering world. But it was enough for North to see the light the darkness will never put out. It was enough for him to find hope for the future. It was enough to lead him to pray:

O Master, from the mountainside
make haste to heal these hearts of pain;
among these restless throngs abide;
O tread the city's streets again.

Till all the world shall learn your love
and follow where your feet have trod,
till, glorious from your heaven above,
shall come the city of our God![7]

The massacre in Bethlehem is an ugly story to include in the Gospel. It is an uncomfortable story that does not leave us with celebration or joy. But it can be a story in which we find hope. It invites us to pray the traditional collect for the day as the church remembers this "slaughter of the innocents."

We remember today, O God, the slaughter of the holy innocents of Bethlehem by King Herod. Receive, we pray, into the arms of your mercy all innocent victims; and by your great might frustrate the designs of evil tyrants and establish your rule of justice, love, and peace; through Jesus Christ our Lord, who lives and reigns with you, in the unity of the Holy Spirit, one God, for ever and ever. Amen.[8]

REMEMBER WHO YOU ARE (AND WHO YOU WILL BECOME)

Matthew 3:1-17

Some days are not ordinary days. They are not like every other day. Ordinary days become extraordinary days because something happens on that day that makes a difference in all the days that follow. Days when we graduate, marry, or give birth redefine the days that follow. Ordinary days and ordinary places become holy days and sacred places because we experience a fresh Epiphany, a new revelation of Christ.

One of those holy days is the day we remember the baptism of Jesus. One of those sacred places is the wilderness around the Jordan where it happened. The Gospel writers agree that a visit with John the Baptist in the wilderness can be a transformative stop along the way of our spiritual journey. The lectionary takes us there every year during Advent on our way to Bethlehem. It takes us back there again on the first Sunday after Epiphany to remember the baptism of Jesus in the Jordan. With other churches that follow the liturgical year, the congregations I served remembered the baptism of our Lord by celebrating both the sacrament of baptism and the reaffirmation of our baptismal vows.

The Epiphany of Christ comes to different people in different ways. For some people, it can be a mind-blowing, knee-shaking, soul-changing surprise. They are *"Bang!* moments"[1] when we suddenly see something we would have otherwise missed. It happened that way for Zechariah. It was an ordinary day in the temple. He was minding his own business, "following the customs of priestly service" (Luke 1:9). Suddenly "an angel from the Lord appeared to him, standing to the right of the altar of incense. When Zechariah saw the angel, he was startled and overcome with fear" (1:12). You'd be frightened too! When I caught my breath, I would probably have said, "Not now, Gabriel! Can't you see I'm doing religious work here?"

After Gabriel calmed the old priest down, Zechariah received the unexpected promise that Elizabeth would give birth to a son who would be "a joy and delight to you" and would "make ready a people prepared for the Lord" (Luke 1:14, 17). The promise left Zechariah speechless. No one was more surprised than Zechariah when the promise became a reality. Elizabeth gave birth to a son. They named him John, and Zechariah regained his voice. John did, in fact, prepare the way for the coming of Christ. The rest is life-changing history, but it began with a shell-shocked old priest who experienced an epiphany he never expected.

Like the story of Zechariah and Elizabeth, most of the traditional scripture readings for the season of Epiphany include the element of surprise. We get the impression that the Holy Spirit's idea of a good time is revealing the extraordinary presence of the Son of God in ordinary places where we least expect to find it.

The Epiphany also comes to people who prepare for it. It is an unearned gift of God's grace at the conclusion of a long and often arduous spiritual journey. The revelation comes as a blessing to people who "[hunger] and [thirst] for righteousness" in the promise that "they will be fed until they are full" (Matthew 5:6). Sometimes the Holy Spirit tracks people down the way Francis Thompson dramatically described God as the "Hound of Heaven."

> I fled Him, down the nights and down the days;
> I fled Him, down the arches of the years;
> I fled Him, down the labyrinthine ways
> Of my own mind; and in the mist of tears
> I hid from Him, and under running laughter.
>
> . . . .
>
> But with unhurrying chase,
> And unperturbèd pace,
> Deliberate speed, majestic instancy,
> They beat—and a Voice beat
> More instant than the Feet—
> "All things betray thee, who betrayest Me."[2]

Wherever we are in our faith journey, the Gospel writers invite us to join the people who found their way into the wilderness where John, the son of Elizabeth and Zechariah, was preparing the way for the coming of Christ. He fulfilled the vision of the prophet Isaiah.

> *A voice is crying out:*
> *"Clear the Lord's way in the desert!*
>   *Make a level highway in the wilderness for our God!*
> *Every valley will be raised up,*
>   *and every mountain and hill will be flattened.*
>   *Uneven ground will become level,*
>   *and rough terrain a valley plain.*
> *The Lord's glory will appear,*
>   *and all humanity will see it together."*
>
>   (Isaiah 40:3-5)

"People from... all around the Jordan River came to him." (Matthew 3:5)

The wilderness is not a comfortable place. John the Baptist is not the friendliest preacher you could find. Clearing the way for the coming of Christ through our crowded, conflicted, chaotic world is not easily done. Making a level highway through the wilderness calls for hard work and a little dynamite along the way. In Luke's Gospel, John attacks his listeners as a "brood of vipers." He commands them to "flee from the coming wrath" and warns them that "every tree that does not bear good fruit will be cut down and thrown into the fire" (Luke 3:7, 9 NRSVue). He proclaims a demanding message of social change and economic justice in the tradition of some of the Old Testament prophets. He calls for repentance as a change in our behavior, concluding with the promise, "I baptize you with water, but the one who is more powerful than me is coming. I'm not worthy to loosen the strap of his sandals. He will baptize you with the Holy Spirit and fire" (Luke 3:16).

John's message is serious stuff! Why would people go to the wilderness to hear a sermon like that? Why would we need to go there?

I'm sure some people simply followed the crowd. They were checking out the latest stories about a wild-eyed prophet by the river. Some were curiosity seekers who were intrigued by the weirdness of John's wardrobe of camel's hair and his diet of locusts and wild honey. Some were spiritual masochists who needed a preacher to tell how bad they were. Some came in response to a divine dissatisfaction with the injustice they saw in their world. They acknowledged a brokenness in their own lives and a nagging emptiness in their souls. Some came like St. Augustine, who prayed, "You have made us for yourself, O Lord, and our hearts are restless until they rest in you."[3] Some came like the prodigal son who, after squandering everything he had been given, remembered he had a father who loved him and got up to return to his true home (Luke 15:11-24).

Regardless of who they were or why they came—regardless of who we are or why we come—they were gathered beside the river when John saw Jesus and declared, "Look! The Lamb of God who takes away the sin of the world!...Even I didn't recognize him" (John 1:29, 31). I'm struck by John's last words. Jesus entered onto the public stage in such an unobtrusive way that even John didn't recognize him at first. He came to the river quietly, calmly, like any other person in the crowd. He came in the spirit of the prophet Isaiah.

> *He won't cry out or shout aloud*
> *   or make his voice heard in public.*
> *He won't break a bruised reed;*
> *   he won't extinguish a faint wick,*
> *   but he will surely bring justice.*
> *He won't be extinguished or broken*
> *   until he has established justice in the land.*
>   (Isaiah 42:2-4)

John was shocked when Jesus came sloshing into the river to be baptized like every other sinner in the crowd. In Matthew's account, John tried to prevent him. He questioned, "I need to be baptized by you, yet you come to me?" (Matthew 3:14).

A young pastor friend described the day his congregation was reaffirming their baptismal vows in worship. He was looking into the faces of people as he daubed some Spirit-blessed water on their foreheads with the words, "Remember your baptism and be grateful." He was surprised when he realized the next person in line was his bishop. He hesitated and felt like saying, "Hold everything! You outrank me. You should be here where I am." The bishop noticed the young pastor's hesitation, smiled, and nodded his head to say, "Let's get on with this. I'm just another sinner standing in the need of grace."

In that spirit, Jesus effectively told John, "Go ahead. Let's do this. It's why I'm here." So John did it! He lowered "the Lamb of God who takes away the sin of the world" into the water, just like everyone else. Jesus was coming up out of the water with dripping hair and blurry eyes when the Epiphany happened. "Suddenly the heavens were opened to him and he saw God's Spirit descending like a dove and alighting on him. And a voice from the heavens said, 'This is my Son, the Beloved, with whom I am well pleased'" (Matthew 3:16-17 NRSVue).

The Gospel writers don't agree on precisely who saw the dove and who heard the voice from heaven. Matthew and Mark describe a deeply personal epiphany addressed directly to Jesus (Matthew 3:16-17; Mark 1:9-11). Luke hangs the revelation out there for everyone (Luke 3:21-22). John's account turns it into a personal witness on the lips of John the Baptist. "I saw the Spirit coming down from heaven like a dove, and it rested on him....I have seen and testified that this one is God's Son" (John 1:33-34). We might wonder who got the story right and which writer was reporting "fake news."

I'm grateful the early church didn't try to harmonize the accounts to make them all come out the same. They didn't give one reading priority over the others or parse the differences to squeeze the revelation of Christ into an "inerrant" text. They passed these accounts on to us the way they received them. The variety affirms for me that the same Epiphany of the same Christ can be experienced in different ways to meet the needs of the people who experience and bear witness to it. The stories have one thing in common: they all declare the unique identity of Jesus as the Son of God.

Remember Who Jesus Is

The overarching purpose of the readings for the season of Epiphany is to remind us that Jesus is the one and only, fully original, ever-living Son of God who, in the words of the Nicene Creed, "For our sake and for our salvation, came down from heaven...and became truly human." The church unashamedly announces the astonishing claim that the infinite God became finite bone, sinew, flesh, and blood among us. This man named Jesus was as much of God as could be squeezed into a human body. In him we see the essential character of the Almighty God. He was, in the words of Charles Wesley, "Our God contracted to a span, / Incomprehensibly made man."[4]

The writer of the letter to the Colossians used the words of an early Christian hymn or affirmation to announce the audacious claim of who Christ is.

> *The Son is the image of the invisible God,*
> *the one who is first over all creation,*
>
> *Because all things were created by him:*
> *both in the heavens and on the earth,*
> *the things that are visible and the things that are invisible.*
> *Whether they are thrones or powers,*
> *or rulers or authorities,*
> *all things were created through him and for him.*
>
> *He existed before all things,*
> *and all things are held together in him....*
> *so that he might occupy the first place in everything.*
>
> *Because all the fullness of God was pleased to live in him.*
> (Colossians 1:15-19)

In his baptism in the river Jordan, Jesus is the Son of God who is with us, birth to earth and womb to tomb, identifying with us in our human failure, sin, and death. Dietrich Bonhoeffer affirmed the radical impact of the Incarnation when he wrote, "God's own image, which had remained with God through eternity, now assumes the image of the fallen, sinful human beings....In Jesus Christ, God's own image has come into our midst in the form of our lost human life."[5] This is a shocking idea, but one that differentiates followers of Christ. We can be religious without the Gospels, and we can be spiritual without Jesus—but we cannot be Christians without them. Although we can never fully explain the mystery of the Incarnation, we can allow the words, will, and way of Jesus to become an internal gyroscope that maintains our balance when everything is changing around us.

I remember the day in a junior high science class when Mr. Marks, our aging and nearly retired teacher, showed us a gyroscope. He set the inner wheel spinning and positioned it on the ring of a water glass. While the inner wheel was spinning, the outer frame kept its balance. When the wheel stopped, the whole thing toppled off the edge of the glass and tumbled down to the floor.

I can't explain the scientific intricacies of the gyroscope any more than I can fully resolve all the questions about the Incarnation. It's a wonder-filled mystery beyond my explanation but not beyond my experience. I am convinced that the love of God that is most fully revealed in Jesus is what T. S. Eliot referred to as "the still point in the turning world."[6] The words Jesus spoke, the things he did, the way he died, and the experience of his risen presence become the still point around which everything in our lives revolves.

Although we can and should debate, doubt, or question those claims, we cannot escape the expansive affirmation that Jesus is the Son of God. But the wilderness is not only the place where we remember who Jesus is. It's also the place where the Spirit of God reminds us of who we are.

Remember Who You Are

One of the humorous legends from the George H. W. Bush presidency is that while visiting a Washington, DC, nursing home, he asked an old man in a wheelchair, "Do you know who I am?" The man gave the president a quizzical look and replied, "No, but if you ask at the front desk, they can tell you."

So, who tells you who you are? We are constantly bombarded by a confusing cacophony of voices that attempt to convince us that our identity is defined by the car we drive, the brand of clothes we wear, the size of checks we can write. Our culture brands us—and we brand ourselves and one another—with labels that can become as divisive as they are descriptive: conservative or liberal, black or white, immigrant or native, straight or gay, Republican or Democrat, young or old. All those things matter in their own way, but the gospel offers something better.

Beside the Jordan, the voice of God breaks through the noisy chatter of our world to remind us of a different, deeper, divinely given identity—an identity that surpasses and transforms every other description of who we are. The God who spoke to Jesus at his baptism speaks the same words to every last, lost, lonely, and infinitely loved one of us, "You are my beloved child, the one I dearly love" (Matthew 3:17, author paraphrase). Eugene Peterson paraphrased those words, "This is my [child], chosen and marked by my love, delight of my life" (MSG). Here's the good news: You are a beloved child of God. The almighty God finds delight in you!

A full-sized billboard beside the interstate exit I take to come home announces, "God is not angry." Sometimes, I'm not sure about that. When I hear the stern warnings from John and acknowledge the racism, dishonesty, greed, violence, political corruption, and economic injustice in our culture, I'm pretty sure God is angry because of the injury we inflict on our siblings and creation. At the same time, the billboard announces good news to people whose religious imaginations have been perverted by joyless, hope-deprived preachers who focus their attention on telling us how bad we are rather than how good we can become along with churches that exclude people who are different than they are. The word spoken over the waters is not just that God loves us but that God delights in every one of us! Baptism is the all-inclusive, outward, and visible sign of an inward and spiritual reality. We are loved and claimed by God as God's own children.

My wife and I have five grandchildren, four through birth and one through adoption. Our daughter and son-in-law were at the hospital when their adopted daughter was born. We were in their home forty-eight hours later to welcome Mattie, named for my wife's grandmother, into the family. Her birthday is a day we will never forget. Two months later, our daughter celebrated the day the judge declared that Mattie legally became their daughter and they became her parents. Our daughter announced the good news on Facebook with these words: "Happy Adoption Day! This was the day the Judge declared that Mattie is stuck with us forever. No take-backs. Love this girl like crazy. Can't wait to see who she becomes. God is good."

The voice of God announces, "This is your special day! You are my beloved son, my beloved daughter. No take-backs. I love this child like crazy." Whether you have been baptized or not, that's who God says you really are.

I've never forgotten a story I picked up as we celebrated our nation's bicentennial in 1976. The Ledford family in Harlan County, Kentucky, traced their identity to the time of the Revolution. Burnam Ledford, the patriarch of the family, was born in 1876 and was still alive to celebrate the bicentennial. He remembered visiting his great-grandmother when he was five years old. She was born in 1791, while George Washington was still president, and lived to be 101 years old. They called her Blind Granny because she had been blind as long as anyone could remember. Burnam remembered her sitting in what seemed to be a very large chair. She called him to her side and drew him up close. She placed her gnarled old fingers on his face, felt his nose and touched his eyes, and traced the form of his face to find out who he resembled. It was her way of saying, "Yep, he's one of ours. He belongs to us." That experience reminded Burnam of who he was and to whom he belonged for the rest of his life.

Remember Who You Can Become

Along the Jordan with Jesus, we are also reminded of who God intends for us to become. In her announcement on "Adoption Day," our daughter named what we feel for all our grandchildren. She not only celebrated Mattie's birth in the past and her adoption in the present. She also looked to the future when she wrote, "Can't wait to see who she becomes."

Not long after Mattie was born, her ten-year-old cousin Julia asked her own mother, "People say that I look like you and Papa. Will Mattie grow up to look like Aunt Deb and Uncle Dan?" That's an intriguing question because Mattie's birth parents were African American. Mattie is Black. Julia's mother wisely answered, "Mattie won't look like Aunt Deb and Uncle Dan, but as she lives with them, she will become like them in other ways."

The Gospels do not describe the physical appearance of Jesus. Most paintings of him usually end up looking like the artist who painted them. But as we live with Jesus, as we grow closer to him, and as we allow his words to permeate our minds and shape our behavior, we can become like him in other ways. The same Spirit who names each of us as God's child is also at work within us to shape and form us into the likeness of Christ and to use us as the agents of God's love and grace in the world.

Bonhoeffer wrote that every follower of Jesus "is given the incomprehensibly great promise that they are to become like Christ.... The image of Christ, which is always before the disciples' eyes, and before which all other images fade away, enters, permeates, and transforms them, so that disciples resemble, indeed become like, their master."[7]

I love the moment in the traditional liturgy for baptism when the pastor looks at the congregation and declares, "Remember your baptism and be grateful." The liturgy is not calling us to remember how or when we were baptized but to remember who we really are because of Jesus's baptism. We are ordinary people who receive the gift of an extraordinary identity as sons and daughters of God and are intended to become more like the Son of God.

Sometimes we hear that voice in the deep silence of our own souls. Sometimes we need to hear it from other people. Years ago, I returned to the small town in Western Pennsylvania where I grew up to attend a family funeral. I saw relatives I had not seen for decades. I had forgotten some of their names, but they hadn't forgotten me. They said, "You're Ves's boy. I knew you when you were only this high." One cousin said, "You look more like your father every time I see you." I did not realize that I had grown to be so much like my father, but they could see him in me.

The painful truth, of course, is that we tend to forget who we are and start believing the voices around us. I have no illusion that the Disney team had scripture in mind when they produced *The Lion King*, but they got the message. The movie opens with a baptism-like scene, when Rafiki lifts Simba, the lion cub, above the rest of the animals. As the son of King Mufasa, Simba is intended to become the future king. But Simba believes the lies of his conniving uncle, Scar, runs away, forgets who he is, and starts living and acting as if he were something less than he was born to be. At the turning point in the movie, Simba sees his reflection in the water and is haunted by the spirit of his father who tells him, "Remember who you are. You are my son and the one true king." Simba remembers who he is. He goes back to claim his rightful identity and to restore the life and health of the lions' pride.

Jesus told his own version of this story. It's the story of a father who had two sons. One took his inheritance, ran as far away from home as he could go, squandered his birthright, and ended up in the pigsty of his own selfishness. That's where Jesus said, "He came to himself" (Luke 15:17 KJV). He remembered who he was. He remembered how much his father loved him. He turned around—the literal translation of the biblical word *repentance*—and found his way back home. His father ran to meet him and welcomed him home to his true identity.

The good news is that when we forget who we are, when we fail to become all that God intends for us to be, the same God who claims us and calls us is the God who saves us. We hear the voice of God, which we had forgotten, saying, "You are my beloved son, my beloved daughter. Remember who you are."

The same Spirit who declares us to be God's sons and daughters is the Spirit who declares that we are also God's servants, sent into the world the way Jesus was sent, to be the agents of God's peace, justice, reconciliation, and love in a world that is conditioned to accept violence, injustice, hate, and death. We are called to become what one writer called "the continuing incarnation," ordinary men and women through whom the extraordinary love of God that became flesh in Jesus becomes flesh again through us. Paul made the same astonishingly visceral claim in his Letter to the Galatians, "My little children, I'm going through labor pains again until Christ is formed in you" (Galatians 4:19).

I was working on a book about Mary, the mother of Jesus, when I was drawn to words from the thirteenth-century philosopher, theologian, and mystic Meister Eckhart. He declared, "We are all meant to be mothers of God." He asked the intriguing question, "What good is it to me for the Creator to give birth to his Son if I do not also give birth to him in my time and my culture."[8] It led me to the conclusion that the gospel is not only about the way we can be "born again," but about the way Christ is "born again" through us. God intends for the same love of God that became flesh through Mary to become flesh again through us. Our experience of the Epiphany of Christ shapes the rest of our lives.

I was nine years old when *A Man Called Peter* was nominated for an Academy Award in 1956. It was the story of a young Presbyterian preacher named Peter Marshall who emigrated from Scotland and became the nationally recognized chaplain of the United States Senate. The movie was one of the early experiences that planted the seeds of my calling to be a preacher.

The movie includes the dramatization of the day Marshall preached in the United States Naval Academy Chapel. On the way to Annapolis, he felt led to change his sermon and took as his text "For what is your life? It is even a vapour, that appeareth for a little time, and then vanisheth away" (James 4:14 KJV). He reminded the midshipmen of the tenuous nature of life, the reality of death, and the promise of eternal life.[9]

Marshall preached that sermon on Sunday, December 7, 1941. No one in the chapel that day knew that while the midshipmen were in worship, the Japanese were attacking Pearl Harbor. It was the last sermon many of them would hear before serving in a war from which many of them would not return.

Hugo Schmidt was one of the midshipmen in the chapel that day, and he never forgot Marshall's words. They helped define who he was and who he would become. A picture-perfect representative of Tom Brokaw's "Greatest Generation," he served with distinction in the navy and returned to Tampa where he met the woman with whom he shared seventy years of marriage. He built a business, raised a family, and became a leader in the community. He chaired the Hillsborough County School Board during the challenging years of integration of the public schools. And he lived his faith.

No one loved his church more deeply or served more effectively than Hugo. He was faithful in worship, led multiple groups in Disciple Bible Study, and served in almost every role of leadership in the congregation. Every pastor who served Hyde Park United Methodist for the next seventy years was blessed by his wisdom, laughter, and friendship. When he died at ninety-eight, we celebrated a life that demonstrated what Marshall preached in the Academy chapel. Hugo knew the tenuous nature of life, made the most of every day, and died in the hope of the Resurrection. He requested that his memorial service include his favorite hymn, "Christ the Lord is Risen Today." C. S. Lewis could have been describing Hugo when he wrote, "The Christians who did most for the present world were just those who thought most of the next.... Aim at Heaven and you will get earth 'thrown in.'"[10]

Remember to Remember

The word *remember* appears 297 times in the Common English Bible. It is most often a command. The biblical writers knew what the editors of *Psychology Today* tell us: "Memory allows us to know ourselves—to develop a sense of who we are, what our lives are like, and why. It is fundamental to a rich sense of self that stretches back to our first years and forward into the future."[11]

My guess is that Jesus never forgot the day and the place where he was baptized and heard the voice of God speaking directly to him, "You are my beloved Son." It was his personal epiphany that rooted him in the past, guided him in the present, and strengthened him with hope for the future.

We know that when the days were long, the crowds demanding, and the ministry exhausting, Jesus went "to a deserted place where he could be alone in prayer" (Mark 1:35). I suspect that in some of those times of prayer, Jesus wondered how he got into this ministry and how he could keep going. In those lonely hours, his memory must have carried him back to the day he went to the wilderness to hear John. He remembered how the water felt when he stepped into the river, how it felt to go under the water, and the surprise when he came out of the water and heard the voice that told him who he was and who he was called to be. The memory of that day, that place, and that voice must have been with him as he prayed in the garden of Gethsemane and on the cross when, "crying out in a loud voice, Jesus said, 'Father, into your hands I entrust my life'" (Luke 23:46).

We cannot live in the past, holding onto nostalgia about the way things were or the way we like to believe they were. But we can remember the past in a way that guides us through the present and can give us hope for the future.

I remember the day and can visualize the place where I was baptized. My family participated in a denomination that did not practice infant baptism. One autumn Sunday morning when I was twelve years old, my parents announced that we were going to the First Methodist Church a few blocks from our home. I'm amazed that I never asked them to explain a decision that would shape the rest of my life. My twin brother and I immediately became active in the Methodist Youth Fellowship. During Lent we participated in a weekly class for youth in preparation for membership. We call it "confirmation" today. To join the church on Palm Sunday, we needed to be baptized. We now believe that baptisms should be included in worship except under unique circumstances. Back then, our pastor, Rev. Ralph Richardson, met our family at the altar rail on Saturday morning. He prayed over us, put the water on our heads, and it was done.

That's all I remember. I did not experience a surprising epiphany. I heard no voice from heaven. The moment had none of the emotion or inspiration of the "altar calls" I had experienced in revival services or at camp meetings in the past. It was simply something we had to do if we wanted to join the church. Across the years I came to a deeper appreciation of the meaning of baptism and of the way the Spirit of God uses it to remind us of who Jesus is, who we are, and who we can become.

When the revised version of *The United Methodist Hymnal* was published in 1989, it included the liturgy for the Reaffirmation of the Baptismal Covenant. I discovered the way repetition of the baptismal vows can form a kind of continuing incarnation in our lives.

> Do you renounce the spiritual forces of wickedness,
> reject the evil powers of this world,
> and repent of your sin?
>
> Do you accept the freedom and power God gives you
> to resist evil, injustice, and oppression
> in whatever forms they present themselves?
> Do you confess Jesus Christ as your Savior,
> put your whole trust in his grace,
> and promise to serve him as your Lord,
> in union with the church which Christ has opened
>   to people of all ages, nations and races?
>
> According to the grace given to you,
> will you remain faithful members of Christ's holy church,
> and serve as Christ's representative in the world?[12]

Whether we can remember the event of our baptism or have never been baptized, the baptismal vows can be the way we prepare for the Epiphany of Christ in our lives.

I remember an Epiphany Sunday when I led the congregation in the liturgy for the Reaffirmation of the Baptismal Covenant. We confessed our sin, affirmed our faith, and responded to the baptismal vows. One by one, people came forward, the way people came to John for baptism. I placed the water on their foreheads and spoke the words "Remember your baptism and be grateful." One by one, they moved on. But one man stopped, looked directly into my eyes, wrapped his arms around me, and said with tears running down his cheeks, "I remember the day you baptized me."

It brought back the memory of the day some years before, when he shared with me the hard path his life had taken. He was ready to start again. It was like people coming to John to repent and turn in a new direction. I baptized him in worship a few weeks later, and he had been following that path ever since. I had forgotten his baptism. But he remembered. More important, God remembered and had been faithful to the baptismal promise.

Some days are not ordinary days like every other day. Ordinary days become extraordinary days because they influence the rest of our days. Ordinary places become holy places because they are places where we experience a fresh Epiphany, a new revelation of Christ. By the presence of the Spirit of God, the Epiphany can make a continuing difference in our lives.

NEW WINE AT THE WEDDING

John 2:1-12

Every wedding day is an extraordinary day for the couple being married. But it's also true that weddings happen every day. On average, 5,660 people are married every day in the United States.[1] So, why does John place the story of the wedding in Cana in such a prominent place at the beginning of Jesus's ministry? And why has this wedding story been associated with the season of Epiphany since the earliest centuries of the church? John answers with the punch line at the end of the story.

> *Jesus did this, the first of his signs, in Cana of Galilee and revealed his glory, and his disciples believed in him.*
>
> (John 2:11 NRSVue)

This is not only a wedding story. This is an Epiphany story. It is the first miraculous, unexpected revelation of the glory of God at the wedding in Cana.

"There was a wedding in Cana of Galilee." (John 2:1)

I can't remember every wedding I performed during my years as a pastor, but I remember the first one I performed in my first pastoral appointment fifty-two years ago. The bride was a quiet young woman who said she wanted a "simple wedding." How often have I heard that before the couple is drawn into the web of the multibillion-dollar wedding industry?

The mother of the bride wavered between nervous excitement and overwhelming anxiety, but the bride's aunt was a force of nature. I remember her as a cross between Martha Stewart and General Douglas MacArthur. She took it as a personal insult that they had not rated the services of the senior pastor and were stuck with the new associate pastor, fresh out of seminary. The fact that this was my first wedding increased her compulsion to make sure that every minute detail was up to her expectations.

Mary, the mother of our Lord, might have been the aunt at the wedding in Cana. A nonbiblical tradition says she was the sister of the bridegroom's mother. Whatever her relationship with the family, she was certainly keeping her eye on the details like the aunt at my first wedding. She was aghast when she noticed that they were running out of wine. It would have been a disastrous breach of hospitality that would embarrass the family and be an insult to their guests.

Mary pulled Jesus aside and whispered in his ear, "They don't have any wine." How we hear their conversation depends on how we imagine the tone of their voices. To our ears, Jesus may sound irritated and disrespectful when he replied, "Woman, what does that have to do with me? My time hasn't come yet." Some scholars soften our discomfort by suggesting the word Jesus used to address his mother was a common, perhaps endearing, expression. Or perhaps, Jesus felt his mother was being a little too pushy. We know that in John's Gospel, Jesus's words, "My time hasn't come yet," always point in the direction of the cross when Jesus finally says, "The hour has come for the Son of Man to be glorified" (John 12:23 NRSVue).

Apparently ignoring what Jesus said, Mary ordered the servants to do whatever Jesus told them to do. There were six stone jars, which were used for the rite of purification to cleanse people of ritual impurity that prevented them from being acceptable to God. Each jar held twenty to thirty gallons of water. Jesus told the servants to fill them to the brim. As things turned out, that would be 120 to 180 gallons of wine! Once when I preached on this story, a man told me, "If you can pull off that trick at Lake Butler, I'll bring a ladle!" The point is that it was far more wine than was necessary and extravagantly beyond anything anyone expected or could ever imagine.

The gobsmacked headwaiter had no idea how the wine disaster was averted, but he knew a great vintage when he tasted it. He went directly to the bridegroom and told him, "Everybody I know begins with their finest wines and after the guests have had their fill brings in the cheap stuff. But you've saved the best till now!" (John 2:10 MSG). The guests never knew the source of the wine, but they also knew it was not the cheap stuff! Only a few disciples experienced the miracle as an Epiphany, a mind-blowing, great-tasting sign of the glory of God in Jesus Christ. And they believed in him.

Another definition of the word *epiphany* is "uncovering." When we "uncover" the layers of the story, we discover that it is more than the account of a miraculous event at a particular wedding on a specific date in a village called Cana. In John's Gospel, the miracle stories are like icebergs at sea. On the surface, this is a beautiful story about an unexpected event that would have turned into a disaster if Mary had not noticed the crisis and if Jesus had not acted to solve the problem. But beneath the surface, the water turned into wine is a "miraculous sign" that points beyond itself to the one who caused it.

The miracle at the wedding in Cana is beyond our explanation, but it is not beyond our experience. Our task is not to explicate how the miracle happened but to experience it. The point is not to identify the vintage of the wine, but to taste it. We are invited to step into the story; to feel Mary's anxiety when she saw the crisis; to be among the servants who filled the jugs when they had no idea why they were doing it; to watch the headwaiter's face when he put the wine to his lips and realized how good it was. With the disciples, we are invited to experience the way the glory of God is revealed, uncovered, made known in the life, death, and resurrection of Jesus.

"On the third day..." (John 2:1)

When John used the phrase "on the third day," he was doing more than putting a date on the calendar. For people who know the rest of the story, the phrase is an unmistakable reminder of Jesus's prediction, "The Christ will suffer and rise from the dead on the third day" (Luke 24:46). The words transport us to the empty tomb. An otherwise ordinary wedding story becomes a resurrection story. The unexpected Epiphany at Cana draws us into the miracle of new life of the risen Christ.

I resonate with Eugene Peterson's expression "practice resurrection." It defines the way we continue to live and grow in our relationship with Christ. Peterson writes, "A lively sense of Jesus's resurrection, which took place without any help or comment from us, keeps us from attempting to take charge of our own development and growth.... We live our lives in the practice of what we do not originate and cannot anticipate.... We continuously enter into what is more than we are."[2]

Whenever and wherever we experience the Epiphany, we are drawn into life that is not something we initiate or control. It is not limited to or confined within the narrow categories of our human assumptions. The glory of God in the risen Christ opens our minds, hearts, and souls to a larger, wider, more expansive world. The watery stuff of ordinary life can be transformed into the rich wine of extraordinary new life in Christ. Impossible things become possible. We become "part of the new creation. The old things have gone away, and look, new things have arrived!" (2 Corinthians 5:17).

I experienced this kind of epiphany early one morning in Sioux Falls, South Dakota. I had been invited to teach at the Dakotas Annual Conference. On the first morning of the conference, I made my way onto the running and biking trail that winds along the outskirts of the city. The morning sun revealed the huge expanse of the Great Plains stretching out as far as I could see. I return to that sight in my imagination when I read the psalmist's words: "In tight circumstances I cried to the Lord. / The Lord answered me with wide-open spaces" (Psalm 118:5).

The Hebrew word translated as "wide-open spaces" means "vast expanse" or "broad domain." It sometimes refers to "Yahweh's celestial abode" and can also mean "salvation." It appears three times in the Common English Bible translation of the Psalms (18:19; 31:8; and 119:45). The movement into "wide-open spaces" describes a miraculous element in my journey of faith.

I grew up in a wonderfully warm but consistently conservative spiritual environment in which just about everyone I knew believed the same things I believed. Over time and through broader experience with people of other races with other backgrounds and perspectives, I have been drawn into a wider, more expansive awareness of the wide-open spaces of God's extravagant goodness. I moved from the "tight circumstances" of a religious legalism that needs to squeeze everyone else into a narrow set of assumptions to experiencing a larger receptivity to others. I am being saved from the sin of a self-centered life to grow into what Thomas Merton called "the infinite unselfishness of God."[3] I am being set free from a life driven by my need for attention into the wide-open grace and self-giving love of Jesus Christ.

Paul described a similar experience when he looked back across his life and named how he had moved into the wide-open spaces of life in the risen Christ:

> In Christ I have a righteousness that is not my own and that does not come from the Law but rather from the faithfulness of Christ. It is the righteousness of God that is based on faith. The righteousness that I have comes from knowing Christ, the power of his resurrection, and the participation in his sufferings. It includes being conformed to his death so that I may perhaps reach the goal of the resurrection of the dead.
>
> It's not that I have already reached this goal or have already been perfected, but I pursue it, so that I may grab hold of it because Christ grabbed hold of me for just this purpose. Brothers and sisters, I myself don't think I've reached it, but I do this one thing: I forget about the things behind me and reach out for the things ahead of me. The goal I pursue is the prize of God's upward call in Christ Jesus.
>
> (Philippians 3:9-14)

Any day can become the third day when we practice resurrection and discover the water-into-wine extravagance of the glory of God in Jesus Christ.

"He revealed his glory." (John 2:11)

Glory is not a word we generally use except when we sing "Mine eyes have seen the coming of the glory of the Lord. Glory! Glory! Hallelujah! His truth is marching on."

Glory is beyond our explanation but not beyond our experience. It does not deny the explanation, but it moves beyond it. It is what we feel when we see a "glorious" sunrise or when our spirts are lifted by "glorious" music. An authority in astrometry can explain the rotation of the planet that causes the appearance of the sun rising in the east, although we know that's not actually what happens. A professor of musician can explain the chord progressions and timing of the symphony. But our experience of either of them can move us beyond explanation into a realm of awe that can only be called "glory." A medical team can explain the detailed procedure of labor and delivery. But when the child bursts into life, the parent's experience goes beyond explanation into a sense of relief, awe, and love that is beyond any explanation. That's glory!

In the Bible, people do not simply say the word. They shout or sing "Glory!" The Christmas angels sang "Glory to God in the highest." In Revelation, John heard "every creature in heaven and on earth and under the earth and in the sea" sing:

> Blessing, honor, glory, and power
> belong to the one seated on the throne
> > and to the Lamb
> > > forever and always.
> > > > (Revelation 5:13)

Congregations that follow the traditional worship liturgy sing the Gloria Patri every Sunday in worship:

> Glory be to the Father, and to the Son:
> and to the Holy Ghost;
> As it was in the beginning, is now, and ever shall be:
> world without end. Amen.

Isaiah promised, "The glory of the LORD shall be revealed, / and all flesh shall see it together, / for the mouth of the LORD has spoken" (Isaiah 40:5 NRSVue). On one hand, glory is our response when we catch a glimpse of who God is because of what God does. But in the water turned to wine at Cana, Jesus revealed his own glory. It is not glory that we acknowledge or attribute to him but the glory of God that is inherent in who God is. In the opening verses of the Gospel, John declares, "We have seen his glory, the glory as of a father's only son, full of grace and truth" (John 1:14). That's glory!

John Masefield was the poet laureate of the United Kingdom from 1930 until his death in 1967. In his poem "The Everlasting Mercy," Masefield takes us down into the darkness felt by the poem's antihero, Saul Kane, a belligerent drunk and womanizer who experiences the expansive mercy and extravagant grace of God. He described his experience with the word *glory*.

> O glory of the lighted mind.
> How dead I'd been, how dumb, how blind.
> The station brook, to my new eyes,
> Was babbling out of Paradise,
> The waters rushing from the rain
> Were singing Christ has risen again.
> I thought all earthly creatures knelt
> From rapture of the joy I felt.[4]

Glory is as intoxicating as wine. Having tasted it, we cannot untaste it. In fact, we will long for more. The great sin of institutional religion is that we sometimes turn the overpowering, intoxicating wine of the gospel into something weak, watery, and insignificant. A greater miracle than the one at Cana is performed any time a preacher takes the glory of God and makes it boring. The gospel was so powerful that when it was first proclaimed on the day of Pentecost, the crowd took one look at the disciples and said, "They are filled with new wine!" Peter had to tell them the disciples weren't drunk but were filled with the living Spirit of the risen Christ.

"You kept the good wine until now." (John 2:10)

You can't blame the caterer for being surprised. I picture him as an English butler in the form of Mr. Carson in *Downton Abbey*. He had been around the wedding business for a long time and knew every trick in the book. If more guests showed up than they expected, he could stretch the pâté and slice the lamb thinner. He knew how to take cheap food and make it taste expensive. And he knew the old bartending trick of serving the good wine at the beginning of the celebration with the assumption that guests wouldn't notice if he served the cheap stuff later.

New Wine at the Wedding

You might call it the culinary version of the law of diminishing returns. It's the assumption that the best things come first, after which things begin to go flat, stale, and lifeless. In a culture that has made a religious cult out of youthfulness, it assumes that the best things come early in life, and aging is a steady process of decline. In the context of marriage, it is the sad assumption that the early days of marriage are the "honeymoon," the idyllic days of perfect harmony and endless joy. "The honeymoon is over" has become a common idiom for the later days when life becomes joyless, stale, conflicted, or boring. We are tempted to look at the past with a sense that life has been downhill ever since.

The epiphany in Cana has the power to turn the tables on the assumption of diminishing returns. When the caterer tasted the wine, he was amazed! It was better than any they had served earlier in the feast, better than anything he could bring from the cellar. He was amazed that the bridegroom had saved the best until last. The glory of God in Christ turned the ordinary assumptions on their head. The miraculous taste of the new wine revealed the power of the God who told Isaiah, "Look! I'm doing a new thing; / now it sprouts up; don't you recognize it?" (Isaiah 43:19). Christ fulfills the promise of the writer of the Old Testament book of Ecclesiastes: "Endings are better than beginnings. / …Don't always be asking, 'Where are the good old days?' / Wise folks don't ask questions like that" (Ecclesiastes 7:8, 10 MSG).

I recently came across words I wrote in 1990, which have become tragically prophetic in the 2020s. Aging baby boomers will recognize the television reference.

> Many of us live as if our best days are in the past. We keep looking back to some halcyon moment, some imaginary good old days, back when Ozzie Nelson was in his cardigan, Harriet was in the kitchen, Eisenhower was in the White House, God was in his heaven, and all was well with the world. Not quite! Those "good old days" were good if you were a white, Anglo-Saxon, Protestant male. If you happened

to be Black, Jewish, Catholic; if your voice had a foreign accent; if you were a woman who didn't fit into Harriet Nelson's apron, the good, old days were the pits.

Frankly, I am more than just a little weary of folks who want to take American back to some imagined golden age in the past. It's high time someone gave us a vision of the twenty-first century, rather than try to recreate the nineteenth.[5]

As we uncover the layers in the story of the wedding in Cana, we catch a glimpse of the prophetic vision of that day when "the LORD of heavenly forces will prepare for all peoples / a rich feast, a feast of choice wines, / of select foods rich in flavor, / of choice wines well refined" (Isaiah 25:6). We see a preview of Jesus's parable of the wedding feast (Matthew 22:1-11). We receive an early hint of the wedding feast in Revelation (Revelation 19:1-10). We experience the water turned into wine at the wedding as the miraculous sign of the wine turned into blood when Jesus said, "This cup is the new covenant by my blood, which is poured out for you" (Luke 22:20).

No one anticipated or initiated the miracle at the wedding. It was nothing less than the alchemy of grace, a joyful surprise, offered without price or demand. At the communion table we receive a miraculous gift that is beyond our ability to initiate, create, or earn by our efforts or goodness. We don't grab or take the bread; we receive it into open hands. The wine is offered to us in the spirit with which Jesus offered the cup to his disciples. Our part is to gratefully receive the gifts of God's miraculous grace.

Horatius Bonar combined all these biblical images in his communion hymn:

> Here, O my Lord, I see thee face to face;
> here would I touch and handle things unseen;
> here grasp with firmer hand eternal grace
> and all my weariness upon thee lean.

This is the hour of banquet and of song;
this is the heavenly table spread for me;
here let me feast, and feasting, still prolong
the hallowed hour of fellowship with thee.

Here would I feed upon the bread of God,
here drink with thee the royal wine of heaven;
here would I lay aside each earthly load,
here taste afresh the calm of sin forgiven....

Feast after feast thus comes, and passes by;
yet passing, points to the glad feast above;
giving sweet foretaste of the festal joy,
the Lamb's great bridal feast of bliss and love.[6]

"His disciples believed in him." (John 2:11 NRSVue)

I once thought "believing" meant becoming convinced of the truth of the faith based on rational arguments or verifiable facts. I assumed that turning the water into wine was all the disciples needed to be sure that Jesus was the Son of God, as if one "miraculous sign" is enough for any of us. But if we read the rest of the Gospel stories, we know that clearly wasn't the case. Even at the Ascension, Matthew recorded, "When they saw him, they worshipped him, but some doubted" (Matthew 28:17). It took three centuries of strenuous debate for the early Christians to nail down the Apostles' Creed. We still don't assume that everyone who affirms it in worship is fully convinced of its truth.

The disciples might have described their experience at the wedding the way David Brooks described the beginnings of his journey from agnosticism to faith. The columnist wrote in *The New York Times* that when faith "finally tiptoed into [his] life," it began with "scattered moments of awe and wonder that wash over most of us unexpectedly from time to time." That's about as good a definition of an epiphany as I have found. He sensed he was "in the presence of something overwhelming, mysterious." That is what most of us would say about the water-into-wine miracle. Brooks continued, "These experiences didn't answer questions or settle anything; on the contrary, they opened up even vaster mysteries. They revealed wider dimensions of existence than I had ever imagined and aroused a desire to be opened up still further."[7]

There was more searching, studying, and thinking for Brooks, just as there is for every one of us. But the Epiphany of God's glory in a glass of wine is a good place to begin. The taste is just enough to make us want more. That may be why John names this as the "first miraculous sign." It gives us a taste for something better and leaves us with a desire for more. Perhaps that's what it means to believe.

During my last decade of pastoral ministry, I was drawn into a group of ten men, all of whom were at least a decade younger than I was at the time. Each man was deeply engaged in his career and family. Each had a different story of his faith journey. What bound us together was a common desire for a deeper, richer, more authentic faith. As we grew in our trust of one another, we shared our doubts, struggles, hurts, and defeats along with our hopes and joys. My memory of that group may be like the way the disciples remembered the taste of the wine at Cana. It left me with a deep desire for more.

It should be no surprise that Jesus's "first miraculous sign" happened at a wedding. Paul had good reason to name marriage as "a great mystery" (Ephesians 5:32 NRSVue). The idea that two people will bring the differences in their Myers-Briggs personality types, the baggage of their pasts, and their divergent hopes for the future into a commitment "to have and to hold from this day forward, for better, for worse, for richer, for poorer, in sickness and in health, to love and to cherish, as long as life shall last" is either miraculous or it is absurd. Our pastor in the early years of our marriage liked to say that two things convinced him God had a sense of humor. One was the duck-billed platypus. The other was marriage. Nothing is more filled with glory of the love of God than sharing the gift of love with another human being. Nothing is more beyond the limited capacity of human love.

Not every marriage I performed has lasted across the years. Despite every effort of counseling and preparation for marriage, approximately 40 to 50 percent of first marriages end in divorce. Some looked like disasters waiting to happen from the beginning, but I never had much luck trying to talk people out of it! Some required radical amputation for each partner to live a healthy life. I knew some of those people long enough to see them through the hard times and perform a new marriage with better hopes for the future. Thankfully, some marriages live up to the high intentions of the liturgy. Gene and Emily Ann Zimmerman were married on Christmas Eve. If he had lived one more month, they would have celebrated their seventy-fourth anniversary. All of us who were blessed to have known them would agree that one of the "miraculous signs" of their marriage was irrepressible joy. We will carry the sound of their laughter with us as long as we live.

It's nothing short of a joyful miracle to see marriages that continue to thrive in old age. I've never forgotten Maynard and Sara. They had been married more than half a century when I became their pastor. I always knew I could find them on the aisle, at the end of the third pew on my right. One Sunday morning during the passing of the peace, I stopped to greet them. Maynard told me that day was their sixtieth anniversary. I asked, "How do you account for the longevity of your marriage?" Quick as a whip, Sara laughed as she replied, "We've never had a gun in the house!" Her response along with their faithfulness in worship suggest that a long-term marriage is the result of careful discipline, consistent faith, strong love, and a joyful sense of humor.

Why did democracy-loving, flag-waving Americans get up early in the morning of May 19, 2018, to watch the wedding of Prince Harry and Meghan Markle? My guess was that in a time when our senses were numbed by relentless headlines of conflict and corruption, polarization, and pain, the wedding reminded us of something deeper, stronger, longer lasting, and more life-giving. It was a momentary taste of the rich wine of love and joy.

The preacher for the wedding was American Episcopal bishop Michael Curry. *The New York Times* asked, "What if the surprise biggest star...of this royal wedding was a sermon about love?" The writer called it "a searing, soaring thirteen-minute speech, imploring Christians to put love at the center of their spiritual and political lives." Bishop Curry challenged all of us: "We must discover the redemptive power of love....And when we discover that we will be able to make of this old world a new world."[8]

The memory of the bishop's sermon at the wedding is a continuing reminder of Jesus's command to love each other as he loved us and to keep his model of self-giving love at the center of our life together.

Put *doctrine* at the center and you can end up with a cold rationalism that places a higher priority on suffocating dogma than on grace-filled relationships.

Put *providence* at the center and you can end up with a distant, micromanaging God who robs us of our freedom.

Put *holiness* at the center and you risk becoming a self-righteous perfectionist.

Put *church* at the center and you can end up with a rigid institutionalism that is impervious to change.

Put *patriotism* at the center and you end up with jingoistic nationalism and a world in conflict.

Doctrine, providence, holiness, church, and patriotism matter. But Jesus commands us to put love at the center (Matthew 22:34-40). So did Bishop Curry. It wasn't just what he said; it was the exuberant joy with which he said it.

The Epiphany that happened in Cana still happens. The glory of God is revealed when the person of Jesus Christ brings new hope and fresh love into the ordinary places of our lives. The grace of God can take the dull, flat, stale water of mere human existence and turn it into the sparkling, rich wine of new life and love. The risen Christ can transform any common thing into "a thing of beauty [and] a joy forever.... Its loveliness increases; it will never pass into nothingness."[9]

TURNING THE WORLD UPSIDE DOWN

Luke 6:17-49

The Epiphany still happens. Wherever it happens and in whatever way it happens, we catch a glimpse of the glory of God in Jesus Christ. When it happens, it may reorient the trajectory of our lives the way it reoriented the journey of the magi.

The revelation may come in the shimmering beauty of a new star or the hint of an angel's song in a dark sky. It may be when we hold a newborn baby in our arms and feel the promise of a new life in this old world. It may be uncovered through the faithful and hard-earned wisdom of old age. It might sustain us when we can barely hold onto the promise that God is with us in the darkness of pain, suffering, injustice, and death in our broken and hurting world. It may be when we find just enough courage to take one hesitant step into the water of God's grace and hear a voice that tells us who we really are. We may taste it the way the guests in Cana tasted it in a miraculous cup of joy, the delicious reminder of an extravagant goodness that is beyond our expectations or explanations.

The Epiphany still happens for ordinary people who meet Christ in unexpected places. It is always a gift of God that comes to us, not something we conjure on our own. We know in a way that is beyond our ordinary ways of knowing that in Jesus "the Word became flesh and made his home among us." We are humbled because "we have seen his glory, glory like that of a father's only son, full of grace and truth." With all our conflicts, failures, doubts, and fears, with whatever faith we can muster, we dare to believe that "the light shines in the darkness, / and the darkness doesn't extinguish the light" (John 1:5, 14).

I was intrigued by Timothy Eagan's account of his "search for faith" along the Via Francigena, the 1,200-mile pilgrim pathway that leads from Canterbury to Rome. His book *A Pilgrimage to Eternity* is a spiritual travelogue through the conflicted history of Christianity in Europe. He never experienced a soul-shaking conversion or awakening, but he learned that "it helps to walk with eyes open—otherwise you miss the breadcrumbs of epiphany along the way." He affirmed words attributed to St. Julian, the patron saint of wanderers and hospitallers, "The way is made by walking."[1]

The Epiphany still happens for those whose eyes are open to see the "breadcrumbs of epiphany" along the way. The revelation becomes reality beneath the feet of people who walk in the way of faith. In the Bible, faith often has more to do with what we do with our feet than with what we do with our brains. It has more to do with the direction our feet are walking than with our complete, rational explanation of it. It is grounded in facts, but it takes a step beyond the facts into the "wider place" of God's expansive grace. Our Old Testament model is Abraham, who "obeyed when he was called to go out.... He went out without knowing where he was going" (Hebrews 11:8). In the Gospels, we follow the first disciples, who heard Jesus say, "Come, follow me," and then "right away, they left their nets and followed him" (Matthew 4:19-20). We start walking, and along the way, we ask practical questions.

What will it look like for me to walk in the way of Jesus?

What practical difference does the Epiphany make in the way I live?

How does the life that became flesh in Jesus become flesh in me?

Those questions may be the reason the lectionary for the season of Epiphany includes readings from the collections of Jesus's teachings we know as the Sermon on the Mount (Matthew 5–7) or the Sermon on the Plain (Luke 6:20-49). Neither is a sermon the way we think of it, as a one-time event, though we use that term to label them. They are carefully composed collections of the most memorable things Jesus was always preaching and teaching. Think of the stump speech politicians deliver repeatedly to underscore the essential core of their agenda.

The settings make a difference. Writing for a primarily Jewish community, Matthew said Jesus left the crowds and went up on a mountain. It was a reminder of Moses going up the mountain to receive the Ten Commandments. Jesus sat down like a rabbi teaching in the synagogue, and his disciples came to him (Matthew 5:1). Matthew's version is longer and digs more deeply into the complexity of our lives and relationships. Even the most disturbing words have a beauty and a more spiritual quality. You can talk or write that way when you step away from the hustle and bustle of the crowds and get away to the expansive silence of the mountains. Even as I write these words, my imagination takes me to the Spirit-soaked silence and creative beauty of the Great Smoky Mountains.

In Luke's version, Jesus meets us at ground level: "Jesus came down from the mountain with them and stood on a large area of level ground." He was in the middle of "a huge crowd of people from all around Judea and Jerusalem and the area around Tyre and Sidon." Luke, the physician, observes, "They came to hear him and to be healed from their diseases, and those bothered by unclean spirits were healed. The whole crowd wanted to touch him, because power was going out from him and he was healing everyone" (Luke 6:17-19). The scene is less tranquil. The crowd is more demanding. The Sermon is significantly shorter, tighter, and more direct. "Blessed are the poor in spirit" in Matthew 5:3

becomes "Blessed are the poor" in Luke 6:20. The Beatitudes contain parallel warnings in Matthew and Luke. It's an oversimplification, but if Matthew leads us toward spiritual formation, Luke calls for social action.

Again, I'm grateful the early church didn't try to homogenize the texts but included both versions in the canon of scripture. Sometimes we meet Christ in the mountaintop kind of awakening we experience in the Transfiguration. Other times, perhaps most of the time, Christ meets us at ground level, where he cuts to the chase and is revealed in the rough-and-tumble of the gritty stuff in our ordinary lives.

With their differences, the purpose in both Gospels is to describe the way we walk when we walk in the way of Christ. Both portray the behavior of men and women who live in the kingdom of God revealed in Jesus Christ. They have chosen to follow the road Robert Frost called "the one less traveled by, / And that has made all the difference."[2]

With that background, I encourage you to put aside this book. Sit down with a Bible in print or audio form. Read or listen to Jesus's words in one sitting as if you never heard them before. When a particular passage hooks your attention, you may want to pause and reflect on it. What is your initial reaction to Jesus's words? Read Matthew 5–7 and Luke 6:9-49.

"Everyone who hears these words..." (Matthew 7:24)

I had just completed a sermon series on the Sermon on the Mount. A man met me at the door with a frustrated look on his face. He blurted out, "I'm sure glad you're coming down off that mountain!"

He identified with a story I told about a small, rural town where, in the week following the 9/11 attacks, purple paper handouts showed up at the local coffee shop, gas station, grocery store, and post office. Each card carried a verse from the Sermon on the Mount: "Love your enemies" (Matthew 5:44). "Do to others as you would have them do to you" (Matthew 7:12 NRSVue). "If you forgive others their sins, your heavenly Father will also forgive you" (Matthew 6:14). The cards turned up everywhere and they got people talking. A guy sitting at the lunch counter in the diner told the waitress, "I don't know what all them words mean, but they don't sound right to me."

If, in the words of Edgar at the end of *King Lear*, we "speak what we feel and not what we ought to say," both of those men may name how we feel. We may not be sure what the words mean, but they just don't sound right to us. We might be just as happy if Jesus had come down the mountain and left all those words up there.

Some things Jesus said are beautiful: "Notice how the lilies grow" (Luke 12:27).

Some are reassuring: "Your Father knows what you need before you ask" (Matthew 6:8).

Some are obvious: "Neither do people light a lamp and put it under a basket" (Matthew 5:15).

Some are disturbing: "You cannot serve God and wealth" (Matthew 6:24).

Some leave us scratching our heads wondering if Jesus has a clue about what it's like to live in our world. I'm convinced that if some of Jesus's words don't disturb us or makes us feel defensive, we haven't really heard them.

E. Stanley Jones acknowledged that "on the first reading you feel [the Sermon on the Mount] has turned everything upside down, but the second time you read it you discover that it turns everything right side up." In 1931, Jones wrote words that are even more true today: "We have lived so long on the wolf-principles of selfishness and competition and strife that the Christian way of unselfishness, of cooperation, and love seems to us a foreign way.... We must now cease to embalm it. We must embody it."[3]

Jesus's words are downright absurd unless they describe a way of living that is consistent with and a preview of the kingdom of God, which is the redemptive will, saving power, and healing love of God at work in human experience and history. The words define the way people who "desire first and foremost God's kingdom and God's righteousness" (Matthew 6:33) become active participants in God's healing and transformation of the world. What appears impossible becomes possible when the same Christ who is revealed in the Epiphany is alive in us through the power of the Holy Spirit.

The Sermon on the Mount has very little to say about *what* Jesus's disciples believe. It's about *how* those who say they believe will behave. Jesus warns, "Not everybody who says to me, 'Lord, Lord,' will get into the kingdom of heaven. Only those who *do* the will of my Father." He promises that everyone who "hears these words of mine and *puts them into practice* is like a wise builder who built a house on bedrock" (Matthew 7:21, 24, italics added).

So, how do we respond to Jesus's words?

We can reject them. We can simply acknowledge that these words don't sound right to us and set them aside.

We can idealize them. We can hold Jesus's words up as a noble idea that is just too good to be true for us today.

We can spiritualize them. We can keep them in some realm of ethereal spiritual truth light-years removed from the down-to-earth stuff of our ordinary lives.

Or if we dare, we can actualize them. We can take Jesus seriously and act as if Jesus was actually describing what it looks like for God's kingdom to come and for God's will be to done in this world. We can behave as if this is the way he expects his disciples to live. We can allow Jesus's words to come down into the plain, ordinary stuff of our messy, broken, sinful world where they become the measure of the ways in which we have sinned and fallen short of the glory of God. We can, if we will, allow the Spirit of the living Christ to actualize these words in our own lives, so that the written word becomes a living word in us.

Jimmy Carter was clearly one of those people who actualized the words of the Sermon on the Mount. He consistently showed us what it looks like to be an unabashed follower of Christ. Diana Butler Bass added her own words to the outpouring of praise after his death to say, "We never proved ourselves as Americans worthy of the dignity, goodness, charity, and prophetic insight of Jimmy Carter....President Carter had a good life."[4]

The concluding words of Carter's Nobel Peace Prize lecture echo a call to a higher calling to a more peaceful world:

> I worship Jesus Christ, whom we Christians consider to be the Prince of Peace. He taught us to cross religious boundaries, in service and in love....But the present era is a challenging and disturbing time for those whose lives are shaped by religious faith based on kindness toward each other....God gives us the capacity for choice. We can choose to alleviate suffering. We can choose to work together for peace. We can make these changes—and we must.[5]

The Epiphany in Nairobi

The Epiphany happened again for me in the summer of 1986 when I traveled with Methodists from 138 countries to Nairobi, Kenya, for the World Methodist Conference. I went largely as a tourist, but it became a formative experience that has continued to impact my life and helped reorient my ministry. During some of the darkest days in the struggle against apartheid in South Africa, Archbishop Desmond Tutu boldly affirmed his confidence in Jesus's vision of the kingdom of God:

> Praise be to God that our God is a God of righteousness. God is a God of compassion. Our God is a God of liberation. Praise be to God that our God is a God who enlists us, all of us, to be fellow workers to extend his kingdom of righteousness, to help change the

ugliness of this world—its hatred, its enmity, its poverty, its disease, its alienation, its anxiety. He enlists us to be fellow workers with him, to transfigure it into the laughter and the joy, the compassion and the goodness, the love and the peace, the justice and the reconciliation of his kingdom as we work with him to make the kingdoms of this world to become the kingdom of our God and of his Christ.[6]

When the reports from South Africa gave little earthly evidence to support his hope, he declared:

And hey, victory is assured! Because the death and resurrection of our Savior Jesus Christ declare forever that light has overcome darkness, that life has overcome death, that joy and laughter and peace and compassion and justice and caring and sharing…have overcome their counterparts.…Praise…be to our God forever and ever.[7]

I was inspired by Tutu's confidence and amazed by his irrepressible laughter. He confronted evil, injustice, and oppression with an exuberant joy that exploded out of his profound confidence in the ultimate goodness and love of God.

A day later, the Rev. Peter Storey, the leader of Central Methodist Mission in Johannesburg, called the conference to celebrate the victory that was yet to be accomplished: "Because Jesus breaks the walls; because Jesus gives a liberty that none can take away; because His Church will be kept faithful to hope.…Apartheid is doomed!"[8]

He described the large, white candle surrounded by barbed wire that stood on the altar at Central Methodist Mission. They lit the candle in worship each Sunday as they called the names of people who had been arrested, were in prison, or had simply disappeared. They prayed for freedom and committed themselves again to be the agents of God's justice and peace in their land. That day began a transformative relationship with Peter that led to my first visit to South Africa in 1990. During that visit I had the humbling privilege of lighting the candle in worship. I met followers of Christ who took Jesus's words seriously in places and ways I had never experienced.

I stood on the street with members of the Methodist Order of Peacemakers who protested the continuing impact of apartheid and forced enlistment in the South African military. I visited a young physician and his wife who, along with their toddler child, moved into one of the informal settlements to serve among people who lived in corrugated tin shacks. I made pastoral calls in the overcrowded flats in the center of the city. I stayed in the home of a woman who started the first integrated preschool. I served at the People's Center, the first integrated eating place in the city. And I listened. I found myself listening to the gospel in ways I had not been listening before.

Peter Storey is now retired, but he continues to make prophetic difference through his books, sermons, and lectures across the country, and as the result of his years as a professor at Duke Divinity School. My relationship with Peter and Methodist people in South Africa continues to draw me into deeper discipleship and challenges me to live more authentically in ways that are consistent with Jesus's sermon.

I invite you to join me in reflecting on four of Jesus's most challenging statements that define who we are called to be as his followers. The first may be the most surprising.

"Be perfect, therefore, as your heavenly Father is perfect." (Matthew 5:48 NRSVue)

I began the process that would lead to ordination in the Florida Conference of The United Methodist Church during my first year in seminary. The application included the unnerving requirement of a sermon based on Matthew 5:48. The context of Jesus's command makes it even more intimidating in our painfully polarized and conflict-soaked culture.

> *You have heard that it was said, "You shall love your neighbor and hate your enemy." But I say to you: Love your enemies and pray for those who*

> persecute you, so that you may be children of your Father in heaven, for he makes his sun rise on the evil and on the good and sends rain on the righteous and on the unrighteous. For if you love those who love you, what reward do you have? Do not even the tax collectors do the same? And if you greet only your brothers and sisters, what more are you doing than others? Do not even the gentiles do the same? Be perfect, therefore, as your heavenly Father is perfect.
>
> Matthew 5:43-48 NRSVue

It was an uncomfortably appropriate assignment for a seminary student who intended to be one of "Mr. Wesley's preachers." Six months before his death, on September 15, 1790, Wesley wrote a letter to Robert Carr Brackenbury in which he named "Christian perfection" as "the grand depositum which God has lodged with the people called Methodists; and for the sake of propagating this chiefly He appeared to have raised us up."[9] To this day, the bishop asks every person preparing for ordination a series of questions that I believe apply to every follower of Christ.

> Are you going on to perfection?
> Do you expect to be made perfect in love in this life?
> Are you earnestly striving after it?[10]

What in the world (literally in *this* world) do we mean by *perfect*? We're accustomed to saying, "Well, nobody's perfect," as the excuse for just about anything we do that doesn't meet our expectations. And, of course, it's true. None of us are perfect if it means scoring a perfect 10 on everything we do. But that's not what Jesus or Mr. Wesley meant by perfection.

The New Testament Greek word we often translate as "perfect" is *teleios*. It describes that which is complete, whole, full grown, or mature. It is the end toward which we are growing. It's a root for the word *telescope*, the tool that brings something far beyond us closer to us. The context makes it clear that for Jesus, the perfection or completion of our discipleship is maturity in love as defined by God's love for us. The Common English Bible uses the word complete. "Therefore, just as your heavenly Father is *complete* in showing love to everyone, so also you must be complete" (Matthew 5:48).

E. Stanley Jones called Matthew 5:48 "the central ideal" around which the entire Sermon "revolves as on a pivot."[11] From this perspective, Jesus's command to be perfect becomes the end or goal toward which we are always walking as we walk along the way Jesus walked, in the way he walked it.

In *A Disciple's Heart*, I defined Christian perfection, or sanctification, as "God's way of love being worked out in human relationships...the goal toward which we are constantly moving...the relentless hope or heartfelt desire that persistently draws us toward something that is always beyond us." I also pointed out that "Christian perfection is not only about the transformation of the individual heart. It is also about the way people with transformed hearts participate in God's transformation of the world."[12]

The goal or end toward which we are growing is to be made perfect in love—not love as a feeling or emotion, but love acted out in our behavior, the love revealed in the words and way of Jesus. Charles Wesley set this desire to music when he prayed:

> Love immense, and unconfined,
> Love to all of humankind.
> Love, which wills that all should live,
> Love, which all to all would give,
> Love, that over all prevails,
> Love, that never, never fails.[13]

At first, the command seems to turn our world upside down. But on second thought, it turns the world right side up. Jesus's second command turns our attention to how we live in the world.

"You are the light of the world." (Matthew 5:14)

Jesus said, "You are the light of the world." What we do is the outward revelation of who we are. Jesus commanded his followers, "Let your light shine before people, so they can see the good things you do and praise your Father who is in heaven" (Matthew 5:16). The words are consistent with the shout of the Old Testament prophet Isaiah, which is always included in the readings for Epiphany.

> *Arise! Shine! Your light has come;*
> *   the* Lord's *glory has shone upon you.*
> *Though darkness covers the earth*
> *   and gloom the nations,*
> *   the* Lord *will shine upon you;*
> *   God's glory will appear over you.*
>   (Isaiah 60:1-2)

A stained glass window in the Laurie Ray Memorial Chapel at Hyde Park United Methodist Church contains the image of Jesus with his hands outstretched above the words "Come unto me." Today it is above the chancel. Jesus's open hands offer an open invitation to all kinds of people to come to the table, receive the bread and cup, and kneel for prayer.

But when the chapel was originally built, the congregation faced the opposite direction. The stained glass window was above the doors that opened directly onto the sidewalk along a busy street that leads into downtown Tampa. People saw that image of Christ and read his words as they stepped out of the chapel into the rush and noise of the city. I often wondered if the original intent was to hear the risen Christ saying, "Come to me. I've already gone before you into the city. That's where you will find me."

Both interpretations of the window are correct. Jesus invites us into the place where we hear the word preached, are baptized into the body of Christ, receive the bread and cup, are bound together in Christian community, and find the energy and endurance necessary for a life of discipleship.

But the Christ we meet in the chapel persistently calls us out of the chapel and into the world, where Christ intends for us to be the reflection of his light of the world. By the power of the Spirit, we are sent as the agents of his healing, forgiveness, justice, and peace in the community beyond the church walls. Christ invites us to become a part of the answer to the prayer for God's kingdom to come and for God's will be done on earth as in heaven. Jesus calls his followers to be the continuing epiphany of his presence in the ordinary, unexpected places where we find ourselves.

The Bible study at the World Methodist Conference in Nairobi was led by Dr. Donald English. I remember the way he named the importance of our witness in the world. He said the world doesn't need salespersons for the gospel. What the world needs are more free samples.

Jesus's third word defines the way we become the "free samples" of his love in service to others.

"I was in prison and you visited me." (Matthew 25:36)

Margaret Palmer was one of the "free samples." She was an energetic, joyful, retired woman with a laugh that was just as real and deep as her faith. She could also be salty when things weren't going the way she hoped. When she made an appointment to meet with me, I knew it would be a serious conversation, though I had no idea where it would lead.

I knew Margaret had been serving as a "chat lady" at the county jail for over a decade. If I asked her husband about Margaret, he would reply with a smile, "She's in jail again."

The "chat ladies" began when Margaret and two other women realized that after years of studying the gospel, it was time to do something with it. They decided to take Jesus seriously when he said, "I was in prison and you visited me" (Matthew 25:36). Margaret remembered how clearly God's call came to her and how terrified she was the first time she heard the iron gates at the jail lock behind her. Their only task was to be present with the women, to listen to their stories, and to pray with them.

Margaret said women she previously would have identified as "trash" became "real people" to her. She no longer saw them as prisoners but as friends. She laughed with effervescent joy when she said, "It was so much fun!"

It was no longer fun when Margret became painfully aware that she was seeing some of the same women repeatedly. They often went back to the same people engaging in the same drugs, alcohol, and petty crimes because they had nowhere else to go. Margaret was convinced God had given her a vision of a home where recently released women would find security, support, and mentoring to begin a new life.

The need was obvious. Margaret's passion was unrelenting. But I didn't see how she could pull it off. She knew I was skeptical. I asked if there was any agency in the city with whom she could partner. She had already checked that out. No one was doing what needed to be done and she was determined to do it. I suggested she gather a few people to pray with her about it, not at all sure than anything would come of it.

As she left the office, I remembered Gamaliel, who said of the early Christians, "If their plan or activity is of human origin, it will end in ruin. If it originates with God, you won't be able to stop them. Instead, you would actually find yourselves fighting God!" (Acts 5:38-39). It turned out that I grossly underestimated both God's vision and Margaret's passion.

In a short time, an amazing group of people bought into Margaret's idea. An attorney provided pro bono legal assistance to create a nonprofit organization. A real estate firm found a house that was exactly what she envisioned. The men's Bible study group in which her husband participated volunteered to do the renovations. They found the director for the ministry among women Margaret had met as a chat lady in the jail. In 2003, Hillsborough House of Hope welcomed its first residents.

Within a decade, the Hillsborough House of Hope was drawing support from across the city and providing the opportunity for a host of volunteers to find their place to serve. At ninety years old, Margaret was still going strong. Rather than relax in her rocking chair, she envisioned an additional house where recently released women could live with their children. She told me she wanted her ashes to be buried in the House of Hope flower garden. She died at ninety-six, but the House of Hope continues to bear witness to her desire to be the light of Christ in one dark corner of the world.[14]

Jesus's fourth word for us marks the beginning of the sermon. We call these words together the Beatitudes.

"Blessed are you . . ." (Luke 6:20 NRSVue)

On the morning after Representative John Lewis died, historian and Lewis's biographer Jon Meacham called Lewis, "A genuine saint. A human being willing to suffer and die for his understanding of the gospel and how that gospel found expression in America of the twentieth and twenty-first century." Meacham summarized Lewis's life in saying, "He was about the beatitudes.... For him love was not an ideal but love as a reality. He was in the streets because of Jesus of Nazareth."[15]

What does it mean to be "about the beatitudes"? Looking back across the way Lewis joined the Freedom Riders, who faced beatings, fire-bombings, and possible death on bus rides into the Deep South; the way he marched fearlessly across the Edmund Pettus Bridge on

Bloody Sunday; and the way he gave himself in consistently courageous leadership in Congress, it's obvious that being "blessed" doesn't mean that life is easy and we get everything we want. For Lewis, it meant being a follower of Christ who put the Sermon on the Mount into practice through his life, work, faith, and witness.

In the Greek text, the Beatitudes are exclamations of joy that turn our expectations upside down. I've tried to paraphrase them to capture that feeling.

"O, the joy of those who know they are spiritually poor…"

"How blest are those who mourn…"

"O, the happiness of those who are meek…"

I imagine Jesus saying, "Hey, look at this! This is what real life looks like; life so alive with the life of God that it can never be put to death. Here's the kind of person God always intended for you to become!" Being "blessed" means finding life that fulfills God's intention. It's not about what we have, but about knowing who we know we are, what we need, and who we can become. It means becoming the person God intends for us to be. The witness of John Lewis and so many others like him demonstrates that blessedness is not grounded in how much we get from life but in how much we give to it. Blessing is not measured by how much pain we escape but by how fully we enter the pain of a suffering world. Discovering the blessed life begins by wanting it—wanting it so deeply that we will be satisfied with nothing less. We might hear the Beatitudes this way.

How blessed are those who know they have nothing, because they are the people who will be satisfied with nothing less than the presence of God.

How blessed are those who know how to mourn, because they are the people God can comfort.

How blessed are those who are humble about what they have, because they are the people who can inherit what God wants to give.

How blessed are those who know that they are hungry and thirsty, because they are the people whom God can fill.

You are blessed! At first, Matthew's and Luke's versions of Jesus's words turn the world and each of our lives upside down. But the Epiphany still happens. The revelation of Christ comes to those who walk in his way. In the light of that revelation, the words turn everything right side up.

"A Non-Traditional Blessing" brings the Beatitudes into our present time. It was written for a student group in 1985 by a Benedictine nun, Sister Ruth Marlene Fox.

> May God bless you with **discontent** with easy answers, half truths, superficial relationships so that you live from deep within your heart.
>
> May God bless you with **anger** at injustice oppression, abuse and exploitation of people, so that you will work for justice, equality, and peace.
>
> May God bless you with **tears** to shed for those who suffer from pain, rejection, starvation and war, so that you will reach out your hand to comfort them and to change their pain to joy.
>
> May God bless you with the **foolishness** to think you can make a difference in this world, so that you will do the things which others tell you cannot be done.
>
> If you have the courage to accept these blessings, then God will also bless you with
> **happiness** because you will know that you have made life better for others;
> **inner** peace because you will have worked to secure an outer peace for others;
> **laughter** because your heart will be light;
> **faithful** friends because they will recognize your worth as a person.

These blessings are yours—not for the asking, but for the giving—from One who wants to be your companion, our God, who lives and reigns, forever and ever. Amen.[16]

The Epiphany still happens. Albert Schweitzer described the way Christ meets us in unexpected places as we walk in the way Christ calls his disciples to go. On the final page of his classic *The Quest for the Historical Jesus*, the Nobel Prize winner, musician, physician, mission doctor, and theologian wrote:

> He comes to us as One unknown, without a name, as of old, by the lakeside. He came to those men who knew him not. He speaks to us the same word: "Follow thou me!" and sets us to the tasks which he has to fulfill for our time. He commands. And to those who obey Him, whether they be wise or simple, He will reveal Himself in the toils, the conflicts, the sufferings which they shall pass through in his fellowship, and as an ineffable mystery, they shall learn in their own experience who He is.[17]

WAKE UP TO GLORY

Matthew 17:1-8; Luke 9:28-36

Have you ever had a dream that was so real that when you woke up you had to remind yourself that it was a dream? Now and then—not so often that it becomes commonplace but often enough to remember it—you may have that kind of dream. It's not a nightmare that makes you force your eyes open to escape it, never wanting to risk a return. It's a sense of something or someone so beautiful and so real that when you realize you're awake, you wish you could go back to experience it again. A therapist who specializes in analyzing dreams may help explain where the dream came from and why it seems so important, but perhaps it is enough to simply receive it as a surprisingly beautiful gift. As something you cannot recreate, the memory is enough to carry with you or to carry you into the future.

The season of Epiphany draws to its close with that kind of experience. The journey that began with the magi who caught a glimpse of a new star and followed it to find a king whose name they did not know builds toward its crescendo on the Sunday prior to Ash Wednesday and the beginning of Lent. Each stop along the way has invited us to experience the extraordinary Epiphany of Christ in otherwise ordinary places among otherwise ordinary people. There is always an element of surprise in the way the revelation is given, but it is always another glimpse of the glory of God made flesh among us in Jesus.

The final scene in the Epiphany drama takes us to an unnamed mountain where Peter, James, and John nearly sleep through an experience of transcendent glory. Was it a dream or were they fully awake? Or was it somewhere in that mysterious space between the two? We are invited to join them on the mountain where we may wake up to the glory of God in the Transfiguration of Christ.

"Peter and those with him were almost overcome by sleep." (Luke 9:32)

Jesus invited Peter, James, and John to go with him to the mountain to pray. While Jesus prayed, they were falling asleep. This would happen again on the night Jesus asked the same three disciples to go with him to Gethsemane. Again, he asked them to pray with him. He told them, "I'm very sad. It's as if I'm dying. Stay here and keep alert with me" (Matthew 26:38). He went off to a secluded place for the most gut-wrenching time of prayer recorded in the New Testament. When he came back and found them sleeping, he asked Peter, "Couldn't you stay alert one hour with me?" (v. 40). He went off by himself again. Again, he returned to find them sleeping. Matthew tells us, "Their eyes were heavy with sleep" (v. 43). The third time it happened he woke them up and asked, "Will you sleep and rest all night?...Get up. Let's go. Look, here comes my betrayer" (vv. 45-46).

The slumber-prone disciples remind me of evocative words from Pulitzer Prize–winning author Annie Dillard: "What is important is anyone's coming awake.... What is important is the moment of opening a life and feeling it touch—with an electric hiss and cry—this speckled mineral sphere, our present world."[1] The sleepy disciples also raise the disturbing question of how often any of us anywhere sleep through the Epiphany and miss out on the experience of the glory of God.

J. D. Robertson was one of our preaching professors in seminary. He was a delightful Scottish Presbyterian who introduced me to lines from Elizabeth Barrett Browning. I've carried them with me for over fifty years.

> Earth's crammed with heaven,
> And every common bush afire with God;
> But only he who sees takes off his shoes,
> The rest sit round it and pluck blackberries.[2]

Whatever the cause, the result is the same. The glory of God is all around us, but rather than take off our shoes in wonder and amazement, we settle for the blackberries we are plucking along the way.

Sometimes we fall asleep like shepherds keeping watch over our flocks by night. We become so comfortable around our campfire that we nearly sleep through the arrival of an angel who comes to bring good news of great joy. It takes nothing short of "a great assembly of the heavenly forces" to shake us out of our spiritual lethargy to hear them singing "Glory to God in heaven, and on earth peace" (Luke 2:13-14). And sometimes, if we tell the truth, we might choose to stay behind with the sheep while the others "went quickly and found Mary and Joseph, and the baby lying in the manger" (Luke 2:16). We realize what we have missed when the others return, "glorifying and praising God for all they had heard and seen" (Luke 2:20).

Sometimes we miss the Epiphany because we are simply too busy to notice it. Like the headwaiter at the wedding in Cana, we can become so preoccupied with the details of the banquet that we nearly miss the new wine when it is passed around and settle for tap water instead (John 2:9-10).

During my second year in my first pastoral appointment, a fellow pastor invited me to be the speaker for a youth group retreat. He was one of my roommates in my senior year in college, and we later graduated from seminary together as well. At the end of the retreat, he said, "I feel like I just got to know you during this retreat. You were always so busy overachieving in college that I never really got to know you." The words stuck with me because there was so much truth in them. With my firstborn, hyperactive, extroverted personality, I was trying to do everything I could do as rapidly as I could do it. I knew a lot of people, but there were very few with whom I built a relationship or allowed them to know me. With the help of a truth-telling wife, some ruthlessly honest friends, and a competent therapist, I've tried to harness that energy into deeper relationships with people and a deeper openness to the presence of God.

The Epiphany can happen anytime. Christ shows up in unexpected places. The whole creation is "crammed" with the glory of God. The question is whether we will be awake to experience it. The Bible provides plenty of examples of people who are disturbingly similar to us.

"The Lord is definitely in this place, but I didn't know it." (Genesis 28:16)

An Old Testament precedent for this kind of experience is the night Jacob spent in the nowhere space between who he had been and who he would become. With a stone for a pillow, he dreamed of a ladder connecting earth and heaven. Angels were going up and down the ladder while the Lord stood on it and promised Jacob, "I am with you now...I will not leave you until I have done everything that I have promised you" (Genesis 28:15). Jacob woke up from his dream and declared, "The Lord is definitely in this place, but I didn't know it....

This sacred place is awesome. It's none other than God's house and the entrance to heaven" (Genesis 28:16-17). The memory of that epiphany would go with him for the rest of his life.

I wonder how often we sleep through transfiguring moments when, if we were fully awake, we might see and experience the glory of God in our lives. I wonder how many times we are so intensely focused on what is temporal that we miss out on what is eternal. I wonder how often we are so wrapped up in our immediate concerns, struggles, hurts, and anxieties of our days that we miss the eternal purpose of God at work among us. The disciples woke up just in time to experience the glory of God in Jesus Christ. The Transfiguration would have been hard for even sleep-prone disciples to miss.

"The appearance of his face changed and his clothes flashed white like lightning." (Luke 9:29)

I cannot offer a scientific explanation for what "really happened" on the mountain that day. If I tried, it could destroy the experience of it. If we were given a scientific explanation for a kiss, we might never do it again! Shakespeare was correct when he had Hamlet say,

> There are more things in heaven and earth, Horatio,
> Than are dreamt of in your philosophy.[3]

The Transfiguration is beyond scientific analysis. The story is not here for explanation but for the disciples' experience and for ours. It's like my experience when I listen to "Appalachian Spring" by Aaron Copland. A competent musician can explain the key in which the music is written, the instruments that are playing, or the quality of the recording. But when I allow the music to do its work in my imagination, it brings back the sights, sounds, and smells of the sun rising over the

Great Smoky Mountains after a rainy night. The experience does not deny the quality of the composition or the discipline of the musicians without which it would not be worth hearing. But the experience of hearing it goes beyond the explanation.

To attempt an analysis of what happened on the mountain at the Transfiguration would confine the infinite God to the limits of finite space and time. We know that what happened touched the lives of the disciples so deeply that it sent them back into the ordinary paths of their ordinary lives with an extraordinary experience of the glory of God planted in their souls. In a finite moment in time, they were given a vision of the infinite reality of God's redemptive purpose that was being fulfilled in Jesus.

The evidence is that there is a widespread hunger for this experience in our culture today. It is not as an escape from reality, but a deeper way of understanding, living with, and potentially transforming the often-harsh realities of our world. I meet people who are bored with bland religiosity, disappointed by shallow spirituality, or offended by political partisanship masquerading as Christian commitment. At the same time, they are searching for an authentic experience of the glory of God, whether they name it that way or not. Some are discovering Christian meditation, spiritual discipline, community, or more mystical expressions of the faith. Some are discovering the presence of Christ in the rich liturgy of the church for worship, baptism, and Holy Communion.

When we become attuned to everyday epiphanies as a way of living rather than merely a day on the calendar or a season of the liturgical year, it has the potential to awaken us to the glory of God revealed in unexpected places. The Transfiguration is the stunning climax to the season that prepares us for what lies ahead in Lent. What happened on the mountain enabled the disciples to see the whole life and ministry of Jesus in a larger, more expansive perspective.

"Moses and Elijah... were clothed with heavenly splendor and spoke about Jesus' departure, which he would achieve in Jerusalem." (Luke 9:30-31)

Jesus was, to say the least, in good company. Moses was the agent of God's liberating power for the Hebrew people when they were in bondage in Egypt and the one who went up on the mountain to receive the gracious gift of the Ten Commandments. Elijah was the last of the great prophets, the one who proclaimed the promise of the Messiah who would fulfill God's saving purpose, the one who was taken up into heaven in a chariot of fire, the prophet for whom the door is still left ajar during the Passover seder.

The appearance of Moses and Elijah placed Jesus in the long line of the redemptive purpose of God. The disciples saw the task Jesus would complete in Jerusalem as the fulfillment of the saving love of God that had been promised by the prophets. Clothed in glory, they talked with Jesus about the way he would go to the cross.

Luke is a master painter of powerful word pictures. The word *glory* comes from the Hebrew root *kabod*, which literally means "weight" or "heaviness." Glory is the weight that measures the inherent value of something. It's what we mean when we measure the value of a diamond by its weight in carats, or we say something is worth its weight in gold. Luke may have been using a play on words to draw a bold contrast between the disciples who were "weighed down with sleep" (Luke 9:32 NRSVue) and Jesus, who would bear the full weight of the glory of God on the cross.

I have a longtime pastor friend whose favorite expression is "Glory!" When he is genuinely happy, he will drag the word in his deep Southern drawl, "Glooory!" Sitting in his office one day, I noticed the word *Glory* sitting on his windowsill. It looked like it had been cut out of Styrofoam. He told me to pick it up. When I reached over with one hand, I couldn't lift it. It took two hands to lift it off the windowsill. It wasn't carved from Styrofoam; it was molded from solid lead. The artist attempted to capture Paul's words to the Corinthians when he spoke of "the eternal weight of [the] glory" of God (2 Corinthians 4:17 NRSVue).

The glory of God revealed in Jesus is not some light, simplistic, ephemeral triumph over the real pain and problems of life. It is more than the widespread glory of God in creation. The glory of God revealed in the life and death of Jesus is the transfiguring power that meets us in the reality of human sin and suffering. It is the full weight of the infinite love of the Almighty God present in the depths of human experience. The glory of God is heavy. It is, in fact, as heavy as a cross. And that, of course, is where Jesus was going.

In the structure of the Gospels, the Transfiguration is the hinge upon which the story swings. The narrative turns away from Jesus's teaching and healing to begin the inexorable journey toward the cross. The Gospel writers are convinced that if we want to know what glory is, we must go with Jesus to the cross. We know the glory of God when we see the very human, broken, suffering Jesus, dying in self-giving love on the cross. There we know the full weight of the glory of God that will be confirmed in the Resurrection. It will become a living reality in us with the coming of the Holy Spirit and will ultimately be accomplished when the entire groaning creation is healed and made new (Romans 8:18-25).

Luke places the Transfiguration immediately after Jesus's unsettling announcement that he would "suffer many things and be rejected—by the elders, chief priests, and the legal experts—and be killed and be raised on the third day" (Luke 9:22). The glory of the mountain comes on the heels of the disturbing call, "All who want to come after me must say no to themselves, take up their cross daily, and follow me.

All who want to save their lives will lose them. But all who lose their lives because of me will save them. What advantage do people have if they gain the whole world for themselves yet perish or lose their lives?" (Luke 9:23-25).

There is no inherent glory in suffering. There is nothing intrinsically noble or holy about the cross. Crucifixion was a horrifying and humiliating means of execution. God's glory is revealed in the way Jesus faced suffering, the way he forgave his executioners, the way he cared for his mother, and the way he assured another victim that they would be together in paradise. Glory is the way Jesus takes into himself our suffering, sin, and death. He is God-with-us earth to earth, dust to dust, from womb to tomb. The Son of God goes with us through life, in death, and into the new life of the Resurrection.

I suspect Paul shocked the Galatians when he declared, "God forbid that I should glory, save in the cross of our Lord Jesus Christ" (Galatians 6:14 KJV). His words inspired John Bowring to write the old hymn:

> In the cross of Christ I glory,
> towering o'er the wrecks of time;
> all the light of sacred story
> gathers round its head sublime.
>
> When the woes of life o'ertake me,
> hopes deceive, and fears annoy,
> never shall the cross forsake me.
> Lo! it glows with peace and joy.
>
> When the sun of bliss is beaming
> light and love upon my way,
> from the cross the radiance streaming
> adds more luster to the day.

> Bane and blessing, pain and pleasure,
> by the cross are sanctified;
> peace is there that knows no measure,
> joys that through all time abide.[4]

When we meet Christ at the cross, we find the love that sustains us in "bane and blessing," when "the woes of life overtake us," or when "hopes deceive, and fears annoy." Christ meets us in our ordinary places of hope and hurt, joy and pain. When we share those experiences with each other, we catch a glimpse of the glory of God.

Several years ago, I was leading a retreat for a men's group from a different congregation than the one I was serving. In the first session, I invited each man to share some fact about himself that the other men in the group probably did not know, something that had nothing to do with his career. I intended it to be a simple, get-acquainted exercise that would take a few minutes and then we would get on to the Bible study I had planned based on the Transfiguration story. But I seriously underestimated the honesty and openness of this group.

One guy talked about a physical condition that has changed the way he lives. The pastor described profound feelings of insecurity and self-doubt. Another member of the group shared the way he had been raised to be a "self-made" man, whatever that oxymoron means. He described the way his self-confidence got in the way of real friendships. One who was obviously the group comic acknowledged the way he used humor to deflect attention away from his feelings. For the first time, he put aside his humor and told them about how his father had died when he was three, how he had grown up being strong and independent, and how hard it is for him to open himself to other people.

Something happened in that room that took us all by surprise. As we shared some of the painful places in our lives, the countenance of our faces began to change. It was as if the whole room filled with light. We sensed the presence of God's grace at deep places in our experience. It was as if, through the cloudy, incomplete understanding of our human knowledge, we heard a voice saying "You are my beloved sons in whom I am well pleased" (see Matthew 3:17). Along the way, we discovered something of the weight of the eternal glory of God.

In the Transfiguration, the disciples experience the glory of God that was so far beyond them they could never explain it but at the same time was so deep within them they could never escape it. They were so absorbed in the moment that they never wanted to leave.

"Peter said to him, 'Master, it's good that we're here.'" (Luke 9:33)

I'm not surprised that Peter wanted to stay on the mountain. He suggested, "We should construct three shrines: one for you, one for Moses, and one for Elijah." If anything was irrelevant at the time, it was organizing a building committee! Luke was kind to Peter by adding, "He didn't know what he was saying" (Luke 9:33), but I don't buy that. I think Peter knew exactly what he was saying. He wanted to settle down on the mountain, away from the stress of the work, the confusion of the crowds, and the danger of the ordinary world. He wanted to escape the looming darkness of the cross. He wanted to stay in the white glow of God's presence and not have to deal with all the messy stuff of real life. Peter did the talking, but I suspect James and John agreed.

We all know what Peter felt. I often experienced the same feeling on the last day of a summer camp with teenagers. I've known the feeling in times of soulful solitude or during hours of laughter, love, and faith with longtime friends or colleagues. It's the feeling that closes in on us as we pack the leftover food from the family reunion, leave the relatives behind, and head for home alone. It's the nostalgia we feel on Epiphany, the twelfth day of Christmas. The celebrations are over. We take down the Christmas tree, pack away the colored lights, and step back into our ordinary world with a hint of apprehension because we know that Lent will not be far behind.

When we experience the Epiphany, we'd like to stop the clock and hold on to that experience for a moment more. Our instinct is to freeze-frame or institutionalize our experience and build a monument to our past. In the Bible, however, dreams of glory are not given to keep us in the past, but to prepare us for the future, just the way the Transfiguration was given to prepare both Jesus and the disciples for what lay ahead. The memory of those transcendent moments becomes a gift that guides and strengthens us while not keeping us imprisoned in the past.

I recently took a journey in my memory back to a mountaintop in my own spiritual journey. Jumonville is named for a Revolutionary War battle site in Western Pennsylvania. It is now a United Methodist conference and retreat center. It's one of the places I went to summer camp as a teenager.

The distinguishing feature at Jumonville is the huge, white cross on Dunbar's Knob, 2,480 feet above sea level. It is sixty feet tall, weighs 47,000 pounds, and rests on a foundation consisting of 183 tons of concrete. The cross arms project twelve feet on each side. It will withstand winds of one hundred miles an hour. On a clear day, it can be seen as far as fifty miles away and has been used as visual sighting for small planes headed into the Pittsburgh airport. It was dedicated in 1950 as "a monument to the Prince of Peace on the birthplace of a great war."[5]

The cross is inescapably present, always looming over everything that happens in the valley below. I remember hiking up the hill in silence for worship, nearly breathless when we reached the top. We hiked back down the hill, back into the ordinary activities of our ordinary lives, but the memory of that journey up the mountain left an indelible mark on my soul.

Something like that must have happened for Peter, James, and John after their journey to the mountain with Jesus. The story appears in three of the four Gospels with only minor variations. The Epiphany left an indelible mark on their souls and became a formative story for their understanding of the identity of Jesus. It's no surprise to me that Peter wanted to stay there. But while Peter was still speaking, "a cloud overshadowed them. As they entered the cloud, they were overcome with awe" (Luke 9:34).

> ## "A voice from the cloud said, 'This is my Son, my chosen one. Listen to him!'" (Luke 9:35)

Peter couldn't stop talking. But the voice in the cloud cut him off. It was the same voice Jesus heard at his baptism, repeating the same message, "You are my Son, whom I dearly love" (Luke 3:22). Jesus on his way to the cross, is God's chosen one. The way of the cross is the way the infinitely self-giving God intends to save and heal this broken and bruised creation. This is the way we will find the timeless love and grace of God in our own time and our own experience. This is the way in which we are called to walk as we walk in the way of Jesus. The voice said, "Listen to him."

The command of the voice from the cloud raises a challenging question. Do we really listen to him? If we listen, what might we be called to do or be? As we discovered in the previous chapter, the words Jesus spoke and the commands he gave are not always easy and they certainly aren't convenient. They rub against the grain of our commonly held economic and political values. His words often turn our cultural assumptions upside down and inside out. Listening to Jesus and doing what he says can be costly. It requires disciplined study of his words and time to wrestle with them in community with other disciples. Listening to Jesus calls us to personal reflection in prayer, faithful worship, and courageous social action.

At this point in the story, Matthew tells us, "Hearing this, the disciples fell on their faces, filled with awe. But Jesus came and touched them. 'Get up,' he said. 'Don't be afraid.' When they looked up, they saw no one except Jesus" (Matthew 17:6-8). Mark says, "The three of them were terrified" (Mark 9:6). That's an appropriate biblical response. My guess is that we would have been too!

We, too, are sometimes terrified of "spiritual" things. We'd prefer to control, limit, or manipulate them to accomplish our purpose, rather than living into them. We hesitate to own the mystery and to allow the vision to reshape, refine, and control us. We bring our convictions and assumptions to the mountain in hope of getting God's blessing on them rather than gazing in awe into who Christ is and what Christ expects of us. We would rather make God into our image than allow our lives to be reshaped into the image of Christ.

It was a surprising and beautiful moment when Jesus, sensitive to the disciples' fear, stepped out of the transcendent light of the Transfiguration and came to them. He touched them, just the way he touched so many of the people he healed. He spoke the words that are the persistent message to people who are called to participate in God's redemptive work in the world, "Get up and do not be afraid" (Matthew 17:7 NRSVue). They will be the first words the women hear from the risen Christ, followed by his instruction, "Go and tell my brothers that I am going into Galilee. They will see me there" (Matthew 28:9-10).

The light faded. The cloud drifted away. The vision disappeared. The Transfiguration was over. "They found there was no one there at all but Jesus" (Luke 9:36 JBP). They were left with nothing but Jesus. That was all, but that was enough. The time comes for us to get up, come down the mountain, and meet Jesus in the ordinary places of our lives.

All we have is Jesus, but when we listen to him and follow his call, he is enough.

Jesus led Peter, James, and John down from the mountain. They immediately found a demon-possessed boy whom no one else could help. Jesus healed the boy and "everyone was overwhelmed by God's greatness" (Luke 9:43). The transcendent greatness of God revealed on the mountain becomes the immanent greatness of God in response to human suffering and need. The glory that is beyond our explanation in the Transfiguration becomes the glory of God in our finite experience when we meet Christ in places of injustice, poverty, violence, and pain.

The Epiphany still happens. It still leads us to meet Christ in unexpected places. A successful businessman told me he was "done with religion" when he slipped into the balcony of Hyde Park United Methodist Church. That step began a journey that awakened a passion in his heart and led him to find his way to serve. During our first lunch together, I said, "I am going on a mission trip to South Africa. Why don't you come with me?" We were both surprised when he said yes! When we returned, he shared his story:

> Two weeks in South Africa changed me. I can't say I loved or hated the experience. I felt both. I saw the cruelty of extreme poverty. I watched as innocent children suffered from the plague of AIDS. I observed the fear induced by xenophobia. But despite these terrible experiences, I witnessed great examples of Christian love. I saw the commitment of healthcare, social and theological caregivers who were dedicated to making a positive difference in an untenable environment. I left South Africa shocked but astonished.[6]

Back in Tampa, his experience led him to became engaged in an amazing ministry that provides housing, food, counseling, schooling, and a range of additional services to people who are homeless and to those at risk of becoming homeless. He said, "It now holds a special place in my life. Every person in my company has volunteered and served there during their tenure. My greatest pleasure is introducing a young employee to the ministry in the hope that they may experience a transformation like my experience in South Africa."[7]

The Epiphany still happens in the lives of men and women who meet Christ in unexpected places, listen to God's words, and follow God in the world. So, what can we take from the Transfiguration story that will help us wake up to the glory of God?

We wake up to the glory of God through the discipline of prayer. It's no coincidence that the Transfiguration happened while Jesus was praying. This is not prayer as a momentary plea for the rain to stop, the traffic to clear, or our team to win the big game. It is not prayer as a personal shopping list that we hand over to a divine delivery person to bring to us. This is prayer as the discipline of the soul by which we enter the presence of God, prayer as the training room for spiritual fitness, and prayer as a growing, intimate relationship with God.

We wake up to the glory of God when we see our lives as a part of the long story of God's salvation. Moses and Elijah enabled the disciples to see what God was doing in Jesus as the fulfillment of all that God had done and promised in the past. We wake up to the glory of God when we see our lives as one part of the ongoing story of God's work of salvation in the world.

One of the great joys of serving a church that had been around for nearly a century when I arrived there was the constant reminder that the work of God began on that corner long before I became part of it and God will continue to be at work there long after I was gone. We are invited to get in on God's action for one moment in time, trusting that the drama of redemption will continue after we have left the stage.

I will not live long enough to see every broken heart healed, every shattered dream restored, every conflict ended, every injustice made right. I will not see every sword turned into plowshares and every spear turned into pruning hooks. I won't live long enough to see God's kingdom come and God's will be done on earth as it is in heaven in our lifetime. But it is enough to know that I had a part in that story and that my life has played a part of the fulfillment of God's saving purpose in this world.

We wake up to the glory of God when we walk in the way of the cross. The gospel says there is no way to know the glory of God that doesn't lead through the cross. The glory of the Transfiguration leads to Ash Wednesday and the forty-day journey to the cross and resurrection. With Jesus's first disciples we discover the full weight of the glory of God as we learn to deny ourselves, take up our cross, and follow in the footsteps of Jesus.

Frances Perkins (1880–1965) modeled a life that followed Jesus in the way of the cross. She became the first woman to serve in the US cabinet when Franklin Delano Roosevelt made her Secretary of Labor in 1933. Her calling to serve others began as a teenager when she was confirmed in the Episcopal Church. She continued to practice the spiritual disciplines of the faith throughout her life. Even during the stressful twelve years she served in the government, she reserved time in her calendar for a monthly retreat for prayer and reflection with the Sisters of the Poor in Catonsville, Maryland.

She was already engaged in the needs of people in New York City when Triangle Shirtwaist Factory went up in flames in 1911. This event killed 146 garment workers. There were no fire codes in the city at the time. There were no extinguishers, exits were locked, and fire ladders were unable to reach the upper stories of the building. The fire traumatized the city and marked a turning point in Perkins's life. "Her own desires and her own ego became less central, and the cause itself became more central to the structure of her life."[8]

For Frances Perkins, following the way of the cross involved giving her life in service to the needs of people who were suffering the economic impact of the Great Depression. She is remembered as a driving force in the New Deal. Her twelve-year service as Secretary of Labor included establishing Social Security, the Fair Labor Standards Act, the Bureau of Labor Standards, and the National Labor Relations Act. She is also credited with saving thousands of refugees by limiting deportations to Nazi Germany.[9] A prayer for the day on which the Episcopal Church remembers her asks, "Help us, following her example and in union with her prayers, to contend tirelessly for justice and for the protection of all, that we may be faithful followers of Jesus Christ."[10]

According to the calendar, Epiphany comes once a year, on January 6. In the liturgical tradition it is a season that extends from the twelfth day of Christmas to Ash Wednesday. But for those who are awake to the revelation of the glory of God, the Epiphany can happen every day any time of the year. We can meet Christ in unexpected places. The revelation is a gift of God to those who live expectantly with eyes wide open and hearts alert to experience the glory of God in Jesus Christ. We live each day in the spirit of Charles Wesley's Transfiguration hymn.

> Christ, whose glory fills the skies,
> Christ, the true and only Light,
> Sun of righteousness, arise,
> triumph o'er the shade of night;
> Day-spring from on high, be near;
> Day-star, in my heart appear.
> Dark and cheerless is the morn
> unaccompanied by Thee;
> joyless is the day's return,
> till Thy mercy's beams I see,
> till they inward light impart,
> glad my eyes, and warm my heart.

Wake Up to Glory

Visit then this soul of mine,
pierce the gloom of sin and grief;
fill me, radiancy divine,
scatter all my unbelief;
more and more Thyself display,
shining to the perfect day.[11]

EPILOGUE (ASH WEDNESDAY)

Remember You Are Dust

We know when the season of Epiphany begins; we know when it ends; but we don't know how long it will be.

Epiphany begins on January 6, the morning after the twelfth night of Christmas, after all the gifts of partridges in pear trees, maids a-milking, and drummers drumming have been given. It reaches its climax in the sunlit glory of the Transfiguration and moves directly into the dark shadows of Ash Wednesday, the beginning of the forty-day journey to Easter. The date of Ash Wednesday changes because Easter is based on the lunar calendar. As a result, the Epiphany season may have as few as four Sundays and as many as nine. In a sense, that's how life is! We know when our life begins. It begins as it began for Jesus, on the day of our birth. It will end on the day of our death, but we don't know when that day will be. On Ash Wednesday, we hear the ruthlessly honest words as the ashes are imposed on our foreheads, "Remember that you are dust and to dust you will return." With all our knowing, we don't know how long our life will be, but we know we will die. So, what difference does the Epiphany of Christ make in how we face the reality of our death?

Epilogue

"In fact Christ has been raised from the dead." (1 Corinthians 15:20)

Every time we stand in worship to affirm the Apostles' Creed, we declare, "We believe in the resurrection of the body and the life everlasting." The affirmation is based on Paul's *tour de force* on the resurrection in 1 Corinthians 15. He acknowledges that if the Christ we met during Epiphany has not been raised from death, our faith is useless. "If the dead aren't raised, let's eat and drink because tomorrow we'll die" (1 Corinthians 15:32). But Paul won't settle for that and nor should we! Paul shouts, "In fact Christ has been raised from the dead" (v. 20). He doesn't try to explain the mystery. The best he can do is draw a comparison with seeds being planted in the ground. "It's the same with the resurrection of the dead: a rotting body is put into the ground, but what is raised won't ever decay. It's degraded when it's put into the ground, but it's raised in glory. It's weak when it's put into the ground, but it's raised in power" (vv. 42-44).

Every comparison is obviously inadequate, but I caught a fresh glimpse of what Paul describes in a hauntingly beautiful YouTube video. I am emotionally moved nearly every time I watch it. It was posted by the Alzheimer's Research Center and has been seen nearly three million times.[1]

During her career, Marta Cinta González Saldaña danced and taught ballet in Cuba, Madrid, and New York. She died in 2019. The video was recorded while she was confined to a wheelchair and only minimally responsive to people around her. She was given earphones and heard again the music of Tchaikovsky's *Swan Lake*. She had danced the role of Princess Odette, Queen of the Swans, many times. The music touches a deep part of her brain that remains unaffected by Alzheimer's. Her upper body becomes erect. Her arms are outstretched, her hands and fingers in the graceful position of a prima ballerina. She looks up. Her eyes brighten as if she is seeing something we can't see. Her face becomes more alive. Her arms begin to sway in wing-like movement and then collapse before her with the music. Inserted into the video are older films of her dancing the scene. They match perfectly her movement. She is entranced with the music and her frail body is reborn for a moment before our eyes. When the music stops, she nods her head and her arms fall motionless in her lap. Her body and face become weak again. When I watch her, however, I feel I've been given an epiphany; a hint of what "the resurrection of the body and the life everlasting" might be.

One of the reasons the video moves me so deeply is because we watched my mother-in-law die from Alzheimer's disease. She drifted away from us a little at a time, but a few things were so deeply embedded in her brain that she continued to repeat them. Like the ballerina remembering Swan Lake, my mother-in-law quoted words of Scripture she had memorized many years before: "I know whom I have believed, and am persuaded that he is able to keep that which I have committed unto him against that day" (2 Timothy 1:12 KJV). If her faith had been with her in this life only, it would have had little value at the end. We could lay her to rest in the assurance that the hope with which she lived was with her when she died and would be fulfilled in the resurrection.

Ash Wednesday is the inescapable reminder that as human beings we are Spirit-infused dust and to dust we will return. We did not choose the day we are born. We cannot choose the day we die. The only thing we can choose is how we will live between them. What will we do with the season of life in which we find ourselves?

The Long Obedience

I am experiencing the inevitable effects of aging. I gave up waterskiing a long time ago! I am dealing with physical ailments that, though they are not terminal, are inconvenient. Over the years, I've faced two major crises that sent me to the emergency room with high-risk conditions. While being grateful beyond words for the years I served in ministry, there's no way I could do the work or keep up the pace with which I lived. The sum is that whatever time I have left is significantly shorter than the time I've lived, and I have less energy to live it.

I visited Waller McCleskey shortly before he died. He was the epitome of a Southern gentleman in the best sense of the word, a deeply faithful Methodist, and a source of wisdom and strength for me in some difficult days in ministry. His last words to me were "It's been a great life!" Whatever lies ahead for me, it's been a great life! I've been blessed far beyond my deserving with faithful parents, an amazing wife and family, strong friendships, and opportunities I never could have imagined. Words have been my stock and trade. With ashes on the horizon, here are four wise words that are signposts that guided me in the past and that I expect to carry me into my indeterminate future.

First, a few lines from Dag Hammarskjöld. Near the end of my junior year in college, the coed who would become my wife a year later gave me a copy of his beautiful collection of self-reflections, *Markings*. These lines also appeared on a wall poster that moved from office to office with me for decades. Beneath the caption "Night is drawing nigh," the martyred general secretary of the United Nations wrote:

> For all that has been—Thanks!
> To all that shall be—Yes![2]

Second, words from Friedrich Nietzsche that were made familiar to Christian readers by Eugene Peterson in *A Long Obedience in the Same Direction*: "The essential thing 'in heaven and in earth' is, apparently (to repeat it once more), that there should be long *obedience* in the same direction, there thereby results, and has always resulted in the long run, something which has made life worth living."[3]

Third, words from Paul that I remember learning when I was a teenager at the old-fashioned Methodist camp meeting my family attended:

> I consider everything a loss in comparison with the superior value of knowing Christ Jesus my Lord. I have lost everything for him, but what I lost I think of as sewer trash, so that I might gain Christ.... It's not that I have already reached this goal or have already been perfected, but I pursue it, so that I may grab hold of it because Christ grabbed hold of me for just this purpose. Brothers and sisters, I myself don't think I've reached it, but I do this one thing: I forget about the things behind me and reach out for the things ahead of me. The goal I pursue is the prize of God's upward call in Christ Jesus.
>
> (Philippians 3:8, 12-14)

Finally, one verse from Charles Wesley. Among so many of his hymns that are the music of my discipleship, the last verse from "Love Divine, All Loves Excelling" points the way:

> Finish, then, Thy new creation;
> Pure and spotless let us be;
> Let us see Thy great salvation
> Perfectly restored in Thee;
> Changed from glory into glory
> Till with Thee we take our place,
> Till we cast our crowns before Thee,
> Lost in wonder, love and praise.[4]

We leave Epiphany and begin the journey of Lent in the dust and ashes of our mortality. We follow the path that leads to a tomb in hopeful assurance of the ultimate Epiphany of the Resurrection.

"He is going ahead of you into Galilee. You will see him there." (Mark 16:7)

George Gage was among the first people I met when we moved to Tampa. He and a couple of other guys would walk around Davis

Epilogue

Islands on Saturday morning and stop at a little restaurant for a big breakfast. The breakfast may have defeated the physical purpose for the walk, but it encouraged great conversation! For George, walking was both a form of exercise and a way of making new discoveries along the way. He and his wife walked together for forty-five years along the hiking trails in the North Carolina mountains, on trips around the world, and back home on Bayshore Boulevard that snakes its way along the Hillsborough Bay.

During the twenty-two years that I was his pastor, I always knew I could trust George's integrity, wisdom, and faithful commitment to the mission of the church. One morning, he finished preparing his lesson for the adult Sunday school class he helped lead, left his Bible open with his check for the offering, and went for a walk. He was making his way along Bayshore when a speeding drunk driver veered off the road, smashed into the balustrade, and hit George head-on. He was killed instantly. His body was thrown into the bay.

Sometimes, when George and his wife were walking together, George would take off at a more energetic pace, leaving her behind. In the memorial service, their current pastor, Magrey deVega, shared the story of a time that happened while they were in England. His wife sent their children a picture with the caption "We're out for a walk. Do you see that tiny dot in the middle of the picture? That's your dad ahead of me." Magrey concluded the sermon with these powerful words:

> It feels like George has now concluded his walk. But in a very real way, he's just further ahead now than the rest of us. You might say he's kind of a tiny dot on our horizon. But he has left for us a trail to follow that he has blazed. A trail that points us to the faithfulness of a very real God, the saving love of Jesus Christ, and is illuminated by his own enduring legacy of love that will live on, in us, as we continue our own walk, one step at a time.[5]

The picture of George walking ahead of us reminded me of the first words spoken at the empty tomb:

Epilogue

> *Don't be alarmed! You are looking for Jesus of Nazareth, who was crucified. He has been raised. He isn't here. Look, here's the place where they laid him. Go, tell his disciples, especially Peter, that he is going ahead of you into Galilee. You will see him there, just as he told you.*
>
> (Mark 16:6-7)

The Resurrection is the ultimate Epiphany. It holds the promise of Christ's presence and the assurance of the new life of the Resurrection. At the end of this season, whenever it comes, we can be assured that the risen Christ is out ahead of us and we will meet him there. We sing that assurance in the Christmas carol:

> And our eyes at last shall see Him,
> Through His own redeeming love;
> For that Child so dear and gentle
> Is our Lord in heaven above,
> And He leads His children on
> To the place where He is gone.[6]

And we pray it in the collect for Epiphany:

> O God, by the leading of a star you manifested your only Son to the peoples of the earth: Lead us, who know you now by faith, to your presence, where we may see your glory face to face; through Jesus Christ our Lord, who lives and reigns with you and the Holy Spirit, one God, now and for ever.[7]

The Epiphany still happens! We meet Christ in unexpected places, and we expect to meet him again.

NOTES

Invitation

1. Elise Ballard, "My Interview with Maya Angelou and How It Changed My Life," May 28, 2019, https://eliseballard.com/2019/05/28/interview-maya-angelou-changed-life.
2. Diana Butler Bass, "Epiphany Now," January 12, 2022, https://dianabutlerbass.substack.com/p/epiphany-now.
3. Alfred Lord Tennyson, "Ulysses," in *The Early Poems of Alfred Lord Tennyson* (London, Methuen & Company, 1899), 205.

Chapter 1

1. Richard Lacayo, "Books: Closing Accounts: Ansel Adams: An Autobiography," *TIME*, June 21, 2005, https://time.com/archive/6673553/books-closing-accounts-ansel-adams-an-autobiography.
2. Howard L. Brown and Margaret W. Brown, "Follow, I Will Follow Thee" (1935), https://hymnary.org/text/jesus_calls_me_i_must_follow.
3. William Stafford, *The Way It Is* (Saint Paul, MN: Graywolf Press, 1977), 42.
4. John Greenleaf Whittier, "Dear Lord and Father of Mankind," *The United Methodist Hymnal* (Nashville: The United Methodist Publishing House, 1989), 358.
5. Rowan Williams, "Eastern Wisdom for Western Christians," interview by Timothy Jones, *Christian Century*, May 4, 2022, https://www.christiancentury.org/article/interview/eastern-wisdom-western-christians.
6. Diana Butler Bass, "Active Epiphany," January 5, 2023, https://dianabutlerbass.substack.com/p/active-epiphany.
7. Henry van Dyke, *The Story of the Other Wise Man* (New York & London: Harper & Brothers, 1899), 74–75.
8. John Wesley, *A Plain Account of Christian Perfection* (New York: James & John Harper, 1821), 26.

Chapter 2

1. C. Michael Hawn, "History of Hymns: 'Every Time I Feel the Spirit,'" May 19, 2021, Discipleship Ministries, The United Methodist Church, https://www.umcdiscipleship.org/articles/history-of-hymns-every-time-i-feel-the-spirit.
2. Elise Ballard, *Epiphany: True Stories of Sudden Insight to Inspire, Encourage, and Transform* (New York: Harmony Books, 2011), xviii, italics original.
3. Dietrich Bonhoeffer, *Letters and Papers from Prison*, ed. John W. de Gruchy, vol. 8, *Dietrich Bonhoeffer Works* (Minneapolis: Fortress Press, 2010), 148.
4. Bonhoeffer, *Letters and Papers*, 152–153.
5. Diana Butler Bass, "Midnight in America," November 5, 2024, https://dianabutlerbass.substack.com/p/midnight-in-america.
6. T. S. Eliot, "Ash Wednesday" in *The Complete Poems and Plays, 1909–1950* (New York: Harcourt Brace & Company, 1971), 61.
7. Personal correspondence.
8. Yolanda Pierce, "The Spirituality of Waiting," *The Christian Century*, August 5, 2024, https://www.christiancentury.org/voices/spirituality-waiting.
9. Ernest W. Shurtleff, "Lead on, O King Eternal," *The United Methodist Hymnal* (Nashville: The United Methodist Publishing House, 1989), 580.
10. Dag Hammarskjöld, *Markings* (New York: Alfred A. Knopf, 1966), 93.

Chapter 3

1. Shakespeare, *King Lear*, 5.3.322–323.
2. Ellen Davis, *Getting Involved with God: Rediscovering the Old Testament* (Boston: Cowley, 2001), 14.
3. Davis, *Getting Involved*, 17.
4. Davis, *Getting Involved*, 19.
5. William Sloane Coffin, *The Collected Sermons of William Sloane Coffin: The Riverside Years, Vol. 2* (Louisville: Westminster John Knox, 2008), 3, 4, 6.
6. Bonhoeffer, *Letters and Papers*, 52.
7. Frank Mason North, "Where Cross the Crowded Ways of Life," *The United Methodist Hymnal* (Nashville: The United Methodist Publishing House, 1989), 427.
8. "The Holy Innocents" (collect), The Book of Common Prayer (New York: Church Publishing, 1979), 186.

Chapter 4

1. John Maudlin, "Europe: Changing the Rules in the Middle of the Game," *Business Insider*, November 26, 2011, https://www.businessinsider.com/europe-changing-the-rules-in-the-middle-of-the-game-2011-11.
2. Francis Thompson, *The Hound of Heaven* (Philadelphia: Peter Reilly, 1916), 23.
3. Augustine, *Confessions*, book 1, chapter 1.

Notes

4   Charles Wesley, "God with Us," in *A Collection of Hymns for the Use of the People Called Methodist* (London: John Mason, 1841), 560, https://archive.org/details/collectionofhym00wesl.

5   Dietrich Bonhoeffer, *Discipleship*, ed. Geffrey B. Kelley and John D. Godsey, vol. 4, *Dietrich Bonhoeffer Works*, 283, 284.

6   T. S. Eliot, "Four Quartets," line 63.

7   Bonhoeffer, *Discipleship*, 281.

8   James Harnish, *Surprised by Mary: How the Christ Who Was Born through Mary Can Be Born Again through You* (Eugene, OR: Cascade, 2024), xvi.

9   Catherine Marshall, *A Man Called Peter* (Grand Rapids, MI: Chosen Books, 1951), 241–242.

10 C. S. Lewis, *Mere Christianity* (New York: Touchstone, 1996), 119.

11 "Personal Memories and Nostalgia," *Psychology Today*, https://www.psychologytoday.com/us/basics/memory/personal-memories-and-nostalgia.

12 "The Baptismal Covenant IV," *The United Methodist Hymnal* (Nashville: The United Methodist Publishing House, 1989), 50.

Chapter 5

1   "FastStats—Marriage and Divorce," National Center for Health Statistics, Centers for Disease Control, updated March 13, 2024, https://www.cdc.gov/nchs/fastats/marriage-divorce.htm.

2   Eugene Peterson, *Practice Resurrection: A Conversation on Growing Up in Christ* (Grand Rapids: Eerdmans, 2010), 8.

3   Thomas Merton, *The New Seeds of Contemplation* (New York: New Directions, 1961), 124.

4   John Masefield, *The Everlasting Mercy* (London: Sidgwick & Jackson, 1911), 77, https://www.gutenberg.org/ebooks/41467.

5   Personal records.

6   Horatius Bonar, "Here, O My Lord, I See Thee Face to Face," *The United Methodist Hymnal* (Nashville: The United Methodist Publishing House, 1989), 623.

7   David Brooks, "The Shock of Faith: It's Nothing Like I Thought It Would Be," *The New York Times*, December 19, 2024, https://www.nytimes.com/2024/12/19/opinion/faith-god-christianity.html.

8   Margaret Lyons, Anna Schaverien, and Jonah Engel Bromwich, "Bishop Michael Curry's Full Sermon from the Royal Wedding," *The New York Times*, May 19, 2018, https://www.nytimes.com/2018/05/19/style/bishop-michael-curry-royal-wedding.html.

9   John Keats, *Endymion: A Poetic Romance* (London: Taylor and Hessey, 1818), 10.

Chapter 6

1. James Harnish, *Finding Your Bearings: How Words That Guided Jesus through Crisis Can Guide Us* (Eugene, OR: Cascade, 2021), 85.
2. Robert Frost, "The Road Not Taken" in *Mountain Interval* (New York: Henry Holt and Company, 1916), 9.
3. E. Stanley Jones, *The Christ on the Mount: A Living Exposition of Jesus' Words as the Only Practical Way of Life* (Nashville: Abingdon, 1981), 11, 15, 17.
4. Diana Butler Bass, Substack note, December 29, 2024, https://substack.com/@dianabutlerbass/note/c-83556224?.
5. Jimmy Carter, "Nobel Lecture" (The Nobel Foundation, Oslo, Norway, December 10, 2002), https://www.nobelprize.org/prizes/peace/2002/carter/lecture.
6. *Proceedings of the Fifteenth World Methodist Conference*, ed. Joe Hale (Lake Junaluska, NC: World Methodist Council, 1987), 168.
7. *Proceedings*, 169.
8. *Proceedings*, 177.
9. Kevin M. Watson, "The Treasure God Has Entrusted to Methodism," March 3, 2020, https://kevinmwatson.com/2020/03/03/the-treasure-god-has-entrusted-to-methodism.
10. "An Order for Admission of Clergy Candidates to Membership in an Annual Conference," *The United Methodist Book of Worship* (Nashville: The United Methodist Publishing House, 1992), 543.
11. Jones, *The Christ on the Mount*, 36.
12. James Harnish, *A Disciple's Heart Daily Workbook: Growing in Love and Grace* (Nashville: Abingdon, 2015), 19, 28, 108.
13. Charles Wesley, "The Beatitudes," *Hymns and Sacred Poems*, vol. 1 (Bristol: Felix Farley, 1749), 38, https://archive.org/details/bim_eighteenth-century_hymns-and-sacred-poems-_wesley-charles_1749_1.
14. Adapted from James Harnish, *Make a Difference: Following Your Passion and Finding Your Place to Serve* (Nashville: Abingdon, 2017), 47–49.
15. "Historian Jon Meacham Remembers Rep. John Lewis: 'He Was a Genuine Saint,'" *Today*, July 18, 2020, https://www.today.com/video/historian-jon-meacham-remembers-rep-john-lewis-he-was-a-genuine-saint-87924293858.
16. Ruth Marlene Fox, "A Non-Traditional Blessing." Reprinted with permission from Sacred Heart Monastery in Richardton, North Dakota.
17. Albert Schweitzer, *The Quest of the Historical Jesus* (New York: Macmillan, 1910), 40.

Chapter 7

1. Annie Dillard, *An American Childhood* (New York: Harper & Row, 1987), 248.
2. Elizabeth Barrett Browning, *Aurora Leigh: A Poem in Nine Books* (New York: Thomas Y. Crowell & Co: 1883), 265.

Notes

3   Shakespeare, *Hamlet*, 1.5.166–67.
4   John Bowring, "In the Cross of Christ," *The United Methodist Hymnal* (Nashville: The United Methodist Publishing House, 1989), 295.
5   "Cross," Jumonville Camp and Retreat Center, https://www.jumonville.org/location/cross-2.
6   Personal correspondence.
7   Personal correspondence.
8   David Brooks, *The Road to Character* (New York: Random House, 2015), 20.
9   The Frances Perkins Center, "The Woman Behind the New Deal," https://francesperkinscenter.org/learn/her-life.
10   "Frances Perkins, Social Reformer, 1965," *Lesser Feasts and Fasts 2022* (New York: Church Publishing, 2022), 229.
11   Charles Wesley, "Christ, Whose Glory Fills the Skies," *The United Methodist Hymnal* (Nashville: The United Methodist Publishing House, 1989), 173.

Epilogue

1   "Former Ballerina with Alzheimer's Performs 'Swan Lake' Dance," Alzheimer's Research Association, November 19, 2020, https://www.youtube.com/watch?v=IT_tW3EVDK8.
2   Hammarskjöld, *Markings*, 89.
3   Friedrich Nietzsche, *Beyond Good and Evil*, trans. Helen Zimmern (N.p.: Millennium, 2014), 46.
4   Charles Wesley, "Love Divine, All Loves Excelling," *The United Methodist Hymnal* (Nashville: The United Methodist Publishing House, 1989), 384.
5   Personal correspondence.
6   Cecil Frances Alexander, "Once in Royal David's City," *The United Methodist Hymnal* (1989), #250.
7   "The Epiphany" (collect), The Book of Common Prayer (New York: Church Publishing, 1979), 214.